# TIMAEUS AND CRITIAS

PLATO (*c.* 427–347 BC) stands with Socrates and Aristotle as one of the shapers of the whole intellectual tradition of the West. He came from a family that had long played a prominent part in Athenian politics, and it would have been natural for him to follow the same course. He declined to do so, however, disgusted by the violence and corruption of Athenian political life, and sickened especially by the execution in 399 of his friend and teacher, Socrates. Inspired by Socrates' inquiries into the nature of ethical standards, Plato sought a cure for the ills of society, not in practical politics but in philosophy, and arrived at his fundamental and lasting conviction that those ills would never cease until philosophers became rulers or rulers philosophers. At an uncertain date in the early fourth century BC he founded in Athens the Academy, the first permanent institution devoted to philosophical research and teaching, and the prototype of all Western universities. He travelled extensively, notably to Sicily as political adviser to Dionysius II, ruler of Syracuse.

Plato wrote over twenty philosophical dialogues, and there are also extant under his name thirteen letters, whose genuineness is keenly disputed. His literary activity extended over perhaps half a century. Few other writers have exploited so effectively the grace and precision, the flexibility and power, of Greek prose.

SIR DESMOND LEE was born in 1908 and was a scholar at both Repton School and at Corpus Christi College, Cambridge, where he gained a 'double first' in classics. He was a fellow and tutor at Corpus Christi and a university lecturer there from 1937 to 1948. His lifelong association with the college continued after he became headmaster of Clifton College in 1948, when he was also made a life Fellow of Corpus Christi. In 1954 he left Clifton College to take up the position of head___ ___ ___ he remained until 1968. In 1___ chairman of the Headmast___ bridge in 1968 he became S___ (now Wolfson) College, and

of Hughes Hall, Cambridge. Desmond Lee died in December 1993.

He also translated Plato's *The Republic* for Penguin Classics.

THOMAS KJELLER JOHANSEN studied philosophy and classics at Trinity College, Cambridge. He is now University Lecturer in Ancient Philosophy at Oxford University and Tutorial Fellow of Brasenose College, Oxford. His publications include *Plato's Natural Philosophy: A Study of the Timaeus-Critias* (Cambridge, 2004).

# PLATO

# Timaeus *and* Critias

*Translated and annotated by* DESMOND LEE
*Translation revised, introduced and further annotated by*
T. K. JOHANSEN

PENGUIN BOOKS

PENGUIN CLASSICS

Published by the Penguin Group
Penguin Books Ltd, 80 Strand, London WC2R ORL, England
Penguin Group (USA) Inc., 375 Hudson Street, New York, New York 10014, USA
Penguin Group (Canada), 90 Eglinton Avenue East, Suite 700, Toronto, Ontario, Canada M4P 2Y3
(a division of Pearson Penguin Canada Inc.)
Penguin Ireland, 25 St Stephen's Green, Dublin 2, Ireland
(a division of Penguin Books Ltd)
Penguin Group (Australia), 250 Camberwell Road, Camberwell, Victoria 3124, Australia
(a division of Pearson Australia Group Pty Ltd)
Penguin Books India Pvt Ltd, 11 Community Centre, Panchsheel Park, New Delhi – 110 017, India
Penguin Group (NZ), 67 Apollo Drive, Rosedale, North Shore 0632, New Zealand
(a division of Pearson New Zealand Ltd)
Penguin Books (South Africa) (Pty) Ltd, 24 Sturdee Avenue, Rosebank, Johannesburg 2196, South Africa

Penguin Books Ltd, Registered Offices: 80 Strand, London WC2R ORL, England

www.penguin.com

Translation of *Timaeus* first published 1965
Reissued with the addition of *Critias* and the Appendix on Atlantis 1971
Reprinted with revisions 1977
This revised translation and new introduction first published in Penguin Classics 2008

1

Set in 10.25/12.25 pt PostScript Adobe Sabon
Typeset by Rowland Phototypesetting Ltd, Bury St Edmunds, Suffolk
Printed in England by Clays Ltd, St Ives plc

ISBN: 978-0-140-45504-5

www.greenpenguin.co.uk

# Contents

# List of Figures

# Acknowledgements

I am grateful to Professor Keith Guthrie, who read the introduction and the translation of the *Timaeus*, and to Mr David Steele, who read the introduction, both of whom made many helpful suggestions.

Desmond Lee (1965)

I began the revisions of this edition during a visit to the Danish Institute in Athens and completed them while holding a Research Readership from the British Academy. I am grateful to both institutions for their support.

Thomas Johansen (2008)

# Introduction

The *Timaeus-Critias* has a central place in Western thought. It served in antiquity as a focal point of Platonism and had a profound influence on the philosophies of Aristotle and the Stoics. Through its doctrine of a creator god it continued to inspire early Christian thought, while in the Middle Ages it was one of the few Platonic texts available for study. Afterwards, the *Timaeus-Critias* fell under the shadow of other Platonic works, such as the *Republic* and the *Phaedo*. Lately, however, the restoration of the work to its rightful place at the centre of Plato's authorship has begun: nobody who wants to be properly acquainted with Plato's thought, or its history, can afford to ignore it.

## The scope of the *Timaeus-Critias*

Many first-time readers will know this work from the story of Atlantis, the ancient empire of vast wealth and power which disappeared into the sea. This story, however, is only one part of an unfinished trilogy which was to include a cosmology, told by Timaeus, Critias' account of the rise and fall of Atlantis, and a speech by Hermocrates on an undisclosed subject. The three are presented as the elements of a single project – like the several courses of a meal, to use Socrates' metaphor (*Timaeus* 17b). Together they are offered to Socrates in return for his account of an ideal state much like that of the *Republic*. To understand why Plato should have invented the Atlantis story – and invent it he did – we need to grasp its role within the larger design.

A good place to start is the *Republic*. In this work, Plato, through Socrates, confronts the view that being virtuous goes against one's own true interests. Socrates tries to show that justice as such benefits us, because it represents a kind of healthy order in one's soul, while injustice is a diseased disorder. Therefore, just as anyone would prefer bodily health in and of itself to ill health, so justice too is preferable to injustice. The *Timaeus-Critias* takes this reasoning one step further. The *Timaeus* shows how the good order of justice and goodness in general is represented in nature, such that if we follow the life of virtue we shall also be following the natural order and thereby be better off than if we go against nature. The *Critias* further shows how citizens of Socrates' ideally just city will, given the support of the natural order, overcome even the greatest of challenges. So we see in the victory of ancient Athens over Atlantis a practical demonstration of how the world – that is Timaeus' world of good order – will sustain the efforts of the virtuous. Plato means thus to demonstrate the prudential reasons for adopting the virtuous life, as conceived in the *Republic*, and silence those cynical voices who would have us believe that a just life is 'for losers'.

The *Timaeus-Critias* as a whole, then, represents a vision of a world in which good order prevails, from the motions of the planets down to the human sphere. Plato's cosmology, therefore, has an ethical dimension: by studying the cosmic order, we can learn something about the good that we need to pursue in our lives. This message may come as a surprise to some. Plato holds that there are in some sense two different worlds, that of 'forms' or 'ideas', which are immutable and intelligible, and that of sensible things, which are always changing and cannot be grasped by reason. The task of philosophy, as we are told in dialogues such as the *Phaedo* and the *Republic*, is to turn us away from the world of becoming towards the study of the forms, those changeless, eternal objects which, Plato thinks, explain and cause everything else. Only so can we become virtuous and happy. So why does Plato in the *Timaeus* appear to think that the world of change now merits our attention and can help us become better people?

The first thing to be said is that Socrates never denies that some aspects of the natural world can display good order. In the *Gorgias* (508a) 'certain wise men' were commended for saying that the cosmos as a whole displays justice and good order. Again in *Republic* IX (592b) Socrates says that there is a paradigm of the just city laid up in the heavens for the wise man to imitate. Also in other works commonly placed, like the *Timaeus*, within the late period of Plato's authorship, such as the *Philebus* (28d–30c) and *Laws* X, it is suggested that the cosmos represents good order worthy of our study and imitation. These recommendations of cosmology may seem to run against Socrates' statement in *Republic* VII that we should 'leave the things in the sky alone' and focus instead on the perfect but abstract motions of geometrical objects. But this statement should be taken in context: Socrates is articulating a programme of study which will turn the philosopher towards the study of eternal being and away from becoming and in this context the study of the motions of this universe is deemed inappropriate. Nothing Socrates says in *Republic* VII is incompatible with cosmology's being a worthy object of study in other contexts. The *Timaeus*, then, is consistent with other Platonic works in recommending the study of those aspects of the natural world that display good order.

The second thing to say is that the reason why the natural world displays good order, and so merits our attention, lies in its dependency on the forms. In the *Timaeus*, Plato presents the natural world as an image or likeness of the forms. In so far as it is a likeness of the forms the world is also intelligible. The notion that the world of becoming is an image of eternal being is again familiar from other Platonic works; but whereas the emphasis in those works, for example in the *Republic*, was often on the world of becoming being a *mere* image of the forms, and therefore of secondary reality and value, the emphasis in the *Timaeus* is on the positive aspects of the world's likeness to the forms. In so far as the cosmos is a likeness of the forms, it is also intelligible. We need to understand the forms if we are to see the cosmos as their likeness. So the forms retain their crucial role in the *Timaeus* as the font of the intelligibility and being of other things.

## The *Timaeus-Critias* and the *Republic*

We are clearly meant to understand the project of the *Timaeus-Critias* as based on that of the *Republic*. Plato presents the accounts of the *Timaeus-Critias* as a continuation of a speech given by Socrates the previous day. Socrates opens with a résumé of this speech, which covers many of the major points of the *Republic*, the description of the institution of the best city and the organization and education of its citizens. Timaeus tells us that nothing is missing from Socrates' résumé of his speech (19b) – at least nothing that we desire to hear. Nonetheless, there are, as compared with the *Republic*, certain striking omissions, most notably, the philosophers' education in abstract mathematics and dialectic. The character of the guardian that comes to the fore in the *Timaeus-Critias* is that of the guardian warrior rather than the guardian philosopher. In making this selection, it may be that Socrates is preparing us for the subject he wants to be covered next, the action at war of his ideal citizens. Here is what Socrates thinks has yet to be supplied (*Timaeus* 19b–c):

> Let me now go on to tell you how I feel about the constitution we have described. My feelings are rather like those of a man who has somewhere seen some splendid animals, either in a picture or really alive but motionless, and wants to see them moving and competing for prizes in an activity which seems appropriate to their physiques. That's exactly what I feel about the city we have described. I would be glad to hear someone give an account of it fighting with other cities in the contests in which cities compete, entering a war in an appropriate way and showing in the fighting all the qualities one would expect from its system of education and training, both in deeds through its actions and in words by its negotiations with its rivals.

Socrates wants to see his ideal city described in virtuous action, in particular, in contest with other cities. It is clear that he thinks that such a description will serve as a demonstration of the citizens' virtue, because it is in action that the virtuous disposition of the citizens will be manifested. More particularly, Socrates has in mind by 'action' military action. Given that the first aim of the guardians in the *Republic*, of which we are reminded at *Timaeus* 17d, was to defend the city against external and internal foes, it is not surprising that war provides a good test of their virtue. By showing the ideal citizens engage in successful military action, the account will demonstrate the appropriateness of their education and training.

Now the Atlantis story is Critias' direct response to Socrates' request: by an amazing stroke of 'luck', Critias knows a story which tells of a war fought nine thousand years before between Atlantis and Athens, which at the time was a carbon copy of Socrates' ideal city. Critias claims that the story is absolutely true, that is, historically factual, and so will serve to 'transfer to reality' the city that Socrates had described 'as in myth' (26c–d). The story has a complicated pedigree which serves to bolster, apparently, its historical credentials: the account was written down in Egypt eight thousand years before and preserved until Solon was told of it there and conveyed the story to Critias' grandfather in Athens. Should we take the claim to historicity at face value? There are several reasons to be sceptical. First, while much is made of the superior way in which the written records of the Egyptians have preserved the memory of the Atlantis war, the records were made a thousand years after the war, and so presumably rely on an oral tradition. Second, as we know from the *Republic*, the Egyptians are known for their mendacity, and Solon is hardly in a position to verify what he is being told. Third, Critias as a boy heard the 'true' account from his grandfather (121d). But again the *Republic* gives us pause for thought: Socrates here emphasized the credulity with which children receive and appropriate 'myths' or 'falsehoods' (*pseudê*). Our suspicion is strengthened by the fact that the children's festival at which the young Critias heard the story, the Apatouria, was named after an act of deception (*apatê*).

Yet it is not difficult to see why Plato would invest the Atlantis story with historical verisimilitude. As the *Republic* (382c–d) shows, presenting morally edifying stories as ancient history

can have certain rhetorical advantages. If we believe that something has happened, we are clearly more likely to believe that
it could happen, and we are more likely to believe that something has happened although it does not correspond with
current affairs if the claim is that it took place in ancient times.
In the *Republic* the viability of Socrates' political suggestions is
treated with great scepticism; it is clear that if Plato can make
us entertain the possibility that a state like the ideal city once
existed and flourished, then we are more likely to overcome
our scepticism as to its future viability. The afterlife of the
Atlantis story shows how very successful Plato was in making
it plausible as ancient history to his readers.

## Cosmology as 'likely myth'

In a crucial passage at 29b–d Timaeus sets out his methodology:
it is one thing to give accounts of eternal being, it is another
thing to give accounts of something that has come into being
as a likeness of eternal being. Of accounts of eternal being we
can and should expect certainty; of accounts of a generated
likeness we should expect only 'likelihood'. Why we should
expect only likelihood from an account of a likeness is not
immediately clear. In some cases it seems that we can be quite
certain of the features of a likeness, also in their relationship to
the original. Knowing the original Mona Lisa, it seems we may
be quite certain about how a copy is similar to and different
from the original. However, Timaeus' thought seems to be that
the cosmos and its model belong to different kinds of medium,
becoming and eternal being, respectively. In such cases making
a likeness is not, as in the case of the Mona Lisa and the copy,
merely a matter of copying features from one to the other.
Rather, it is a question of finding features for the likeness that
are analogous to those of the original. One might think of
translating a work of literature into music, as did Beethoven in
his *Coriolanus* overture. Timaeus' point would be, then, that
since the cosmos is a likeness which has been made in a fundamentally different medium from its original, there can be no
certainty but only likelihood in showing how its features

resemble those of its model. Timaeus' account of time (37c–d) illustrates the point. The model for the cosmos is eternal; the maker sought to make the cosmos like its model also in this respect; but no created thing can be eternal; so instead he created time as 'an eternal image, progressing according to number, of an eternity that rests in unity' (37d). Time, then, makes the cosmos like its model in so far as it is an analogue in the medium of becoming to the eternity that characterizes being.

One way in which Greek thinkers marked the cognitive status of an account was through the contrast between *logos* and *muthos*, between 'reason' and 'myth', as the words are often rendered. This common contrast is invoked in the characterization of the Atlantis account as *true logos* rather than *muthos* (cf. 20d, 26c–d, 26e). Surprisingly, perhaps, Timaeus chooses both words for his account, for we might have expected him like other thinkers to label his own theory '*logos*' and his opponents' '*muthos*'. So why does he use both terms? One view is that the *logos*/*muthos* contrast stops being significant for Timaeus once he has characterized his account as 'likely'. But that doesn't explain why Timaeus does not simply use a generic word for 'account' (*logos* again on its own would do the job), particularly so soon after Critias and Socrates have used *muthos* to contrast with *logos*. Another option is that Timaeus does mean to downgrade his account compared to other possible accounts when he calls his account a 'likely *muthos*'. It is not hard to see the motivation for such a downgrading since on the three occasions when Timaeus employs the expression, he is explicitly or implicitly comparing the accounts available to humans and gods. So the likely *muthos* is the account which is to be accepted by us as the most likely available to humans, but which may be less likely than the most likely account available to god. Timaeus is showing epistemic humility in the Socratic vein when he calls his own account '*muthos*'.

# The principles of cosmology

Principles are those propositions or entities we need to grasp first in order to understand a body of knowledge. For Plato cosmology is ordered under at least two principles. The basic cause of the cosmos is the divine craftsman or 'demiurge' whose idea it was to create the world. God is without envy and so does not begrudge others the good he himself enjoys. He therefore set out to make another thing as much like himself as possible, that is, as good as possible. His creation follows this principle, the desire to make the world as good as possible. When we seek to explain the way the cosmos is composed we therefore need to grasp the way in which a benevolent agent would make it so as to be as good as possible. The notion that things are to be explained with reference to an end is known as 'teleology'. The cosmology of the *Timaeus* is teleological in that it seeks to explain the cosmos as organized for an end, namely, in order for it to be as good as possible.

By making the basic principle of cosmology teleological, Timaeus is following the demand made by Socrates in the *Phaedo* (97d–98b) that any cosmological account should show why the actual arrangement of the cosmos and its parts is for the best. So, for example, an account of the earth's position should show why it is best for it to be where it is, both for itself and in the larger scheme of things. At the same time, Socrates is objecting to accounts of the cosmos which state the material processes by which a state of affairs comes about as its proper cause (*aitia*). It is clear that he takes this criticism to apply to a large part of natural philosophy as hitherto practised. Timaeus follows suit: he distinguishes the cause of the cosmic order, god's desire for the world to be as good as possible, from what he calls its 'co-causes' (*sunaitia*), the physical processes by which the good is realized, and he, like Socrates, gives explanatory priority to the teleological cause over the material processes (*Timaeus* 46d–e), criticizing those, the majority, who take such unintelligent processes to be proper causes. The emphasis on intelligent causation is, then, both in the *Phaedo* and the *Timaeus* the key to Plato's view of causation and to his criticism of earlier natural philosophy.[1]

The other principle of cosmology relates to the co-causes: it is that of 'necessity'. By necessity we should understand the manner in which certain things follow certain other things. So, for example, for Timaeus fire is necessarily mobile because it is composed of small pyramid-shaped parts, earth is necessarily stable because it is composed of larger cubic parts (*Timaeus* 55e–56a). Or a head covered in less flesh is necessarily more sensitive to impressions than a head cushioned by thick flesh (75a–b). Such necessary conjunctions or consequences of properties are, as it were, brute facts of nature, which god can do nothing to circumvent. God can work with necessity so as to make it serve his purposes: so he can create a human head covered in less flesh in order to maximize our sensitivity, where sensitivity is something good. When necessity works in this way to further the good, we can refer to it as a 'co-cause', for then it contributes to the intelligent cause. But god cannot alter the way necessity itself works. Necessity therefore constitutes a distinct principle of causation which cannot be reduced to teleology. The cosmos as a whole is the result, as Timaeus says, of intelligence persuading necessity for the most part to work for the best. But only for the most part: there remain in the world manifestations of unpersuaded necessity, not working for the good. The cosmos may be the best possible world, but not in a Panglossian sense.

## The *Timaeus*' debt to Presocratic natural philosophy

The *Timaeus* was written against the background of some two hundred years of inquiry into nature by Greek thinkers. The work's relationship to this tradition is one of both debt and innovation. On the one hand, Plato distances himself from certain of his predecessors' explanatory principles. So we saw Socrates in the *Phaedo* criticize those who identify the causes of natural phenomena with material processes. This criticism is reiterated in the *Timaeus* (see in particular 46c–e), where

Timaeus insists that material processes are only properly explanatory in so far as they serve an intelligence which works with a view to the good. Yet, given the right explanatory framework, Timaeus is quite happy, it seems, to adapt a number of Presocratic theories. Examples of such adaptations in the *Timaeus* are numerous. Let us consider just three here. First, Anaxagoras was criticized in the *Phaedo* for not making use of his intelligence (*nous*) but instead resorting to material processes in explaining the ordering of the cosmos. Timaeus takes over Anaxagoras' intelligence, and the idea that it governs the cosmos by revolving (cf. 58a), but he makes sure to show how such circular motion is at the same time the appropriate motion of intelligent thinking. Second, Empedocles has an influence on a range of accounts in the Timaeus, from the claim that there are *four* simple bodies, earth, water, air and fire (31b–32c), to the theory of respiration (79a ff.), and the theory of vision (45b–d). For Timaeus vision takes place by means of fire going out of the eye through its fine-webbed surface, which with the external light forms a single body, which in turn is affected by fiery particles from the sense objects. All of this echoes Empedocles; yet again Timaeus recasts the material processes as the instrument of intelligent causation: vision is constituted in *this* way so as to help us observe the illuminated heavenly bodies, thereby promoting our understanding of the cosmic order (47a–b). Third, Timaeus takes over from Democritus an atomistic conception of the basic constituents of matter. The composition and interaction of bodies are understood in terms of the aggregation and coming apart of atoms. Yet Timaeus' geometrical conception of the atoms points to teleology in a way which sets his theory apart from the atomists': particular triangles are chosen as the constituents of matter because of their beauty (53e) and proportionality with each other (31b–32c, 56c). While atomism for Democritus shows how the appearances of design in the cosmos are illusory, atomism for Timaeus shows the pervasiveness of intelligent order from the universe as a whole down to its smallest constituents. It is often difficult to find *exact* parallels between Timaeus' accounts and his predecessors', but the influence is undeniable. We might even describe Timaeus' cosmology as a patchwork of Presocratic influences woven so as to represent an intelligently ordered, and distinctly Platonic, universe.

## God

For Timaeus the first principle of cosmology is a teleological one: it refers to the good that the cosmos is organized to possess. However, this good does not work as a cause on its own but rather as an object of god's desire. Other teleological theories of nature allow for the good to work as a cause without reference to desires or intentions. So Aristotle holds that there are ends or goals that work in nature without a mind that wants to bring them about. When an acorn, for example, grows to become an oak tree, we can say that it grows *in order to* achieve the end of being an oak tree. Clearly the acorn does not become an oak tree because it wants to, in the way that I go to the bakery because I want bread. For Plato, however, the ends that operate in nature do work as ends, ultimately at least, because they are the objects of god's desire. Plato does not therefore have a natural teleology in Aristotle's sense.

What or who is god such that his desires can bring about the good of the cosmos? The claim that the basic principle of the cosmos is the maker's desire to make the world as good as possible goes hand in hand with the conception of him as a perfect intelligence. As intelligence, he has a complete grasp of the eternal being that serves as his model for the universe, and as intelligence he understands the best way of realizing this model in a world of change. Also as intelligence, god has rational desires, which explain why he would want to set about making the world. Ascribing desires to a 'pure' intelligence might come as a bit of a surprise to us. We are accustomed to the thought, associated with the Scottish philosopher David Hume, that reason on its own does not move anything, but rather requires the presence of desire as a distinct factor in causing action. Plato disagrees: for him part of what it is to have rationality is itself to have certain desires for the good. On this view, we can understand why god as intelligence should also be able to move the world.

God is essential to our understanding of how the world came about. Yet there are other views of Plato's cosmology which see no need for a separate divine creator. Because of their wide influence these views need to be briefly reviewed here. One claim is that the divine demiurge is the same as the world-soul. Such a view has the apparent advantage that it explains how god governs the world since god would be immanent and part of the world. It also avoids the reduplication of rational principles that seem to lie in both having a demiurge and the world-soul control the world's motions.[2] However, the problem with this claim is that Timaeus says that the demiurge and the world-soul belong to different ontological categories, that is 'being' and 'becoming', and so they cannot be the same. On another reading, the demiurge is the same as the forms, that is to say, the intelligible paradigm on which the world is modelled. Perhaps the strongest evidence for this reading is the fact that Timaeus lists only three kinds of entity as required for his cosmology (50c–d): what comes into being, that in which it comes into being, and that from which it comes into being by imitation, i.e. the forms. The latter is then likened to a 'father' (50d), a term that was previously used for the demiurge (28c). So, it seems, we should really think of the forms as the maker of the cosmos. The conclusion does not follow, however. The list of three kinds is not the kind of list on which we should expect the demiurge to appear (just as the list of two kinds at 27d–28a was given alongside the mention of the demiurge). The three kinds are the elements, as it were, needed for the demiurge to do his job; they are distinct from the list of the two causes, divine providence and necessity, which are the first principles of cosmology. One might compare the elements with the ingredients and recipe of a cake, and the chef and his kitchen tools with the first principles; these are different factors in the making of a cake, just as the three kinds and the two principles play different roles in the cosmogony.

Attempts to reduce away the demiurge typically come with a

view of the creation story as a fiction told 'for the sake of instruction', as some ancient philosophers put it.[3] So one implication of the view that the demiurge is the same as the forms is that the world is eternal. For since the three kinds have always been present, as Timaeus claims, and the forms are the demiurge, there is no reason why the forms should not always have been creating the world. When Timaeus describes the chaos that 'used to' obtain before the creation of the cosmos, he must, on this reading, mean simply the state the world would have been in if it had not been ordered by the forms. The temporal 'before and after' is simply window-dressing: there never was a time of chaos before the cosmos was created. Instead, we should take before and after in causal terms: the demiurge, i.e. the forms, was there before the cosmos, just in the sense that the cosmos always depends on their causal agency. The reading will take succour from Timaeus' claim that time only came into being with the universe: so it does not make sense anyway to talk of something that was the case 'before' the universe came into being.

There are passages, however, where the temporal order cannot well be reduced to a causal order (cf., in particular, 34c). But more fundamentally, the reading that identifies the forms with the demiurge seems to undermine the causal model that Plato has made the basis for his entire cosmology, that of craftsmanship. On Plato's model, a genuine craftsman makes his work by looking to a formal model, for example, as in *Republic* X, the form of a couch. He then chooses his materials and works out a likeness of the form in them in the best and finest possible way. In this way, he makes something new come into being that wasn't there before. Two points need to be emphasized here. First, the craftsman is a distinct explanatory factor from the form towards which he looks: the craftsman is not the form of couch. True, he may in some sense be 'informed' by the form of couch, for it is so to speak the form that tells him what the couch is that he is going to make; but it is still because he is *thinking* about and *acting on* that information that a couch comes about. The divine craftsman cannot therefore be reduced to the formal paradigm that he uses in fashioning the world. Second, the formal paradigm is often not enough to explain the way the craftsman makes his artefact. For he has to make a range of creative choices about how the formal paradigm is best implemented, based on other information, such as the characteristics of the available materials. Such decisions are the outcome of practical reasoning, which uses information beyond that conveyed by the formal paradigm. Since, then, the demiurge also engages in such practical reasoning, his activities cannot be exhaustively explained in terms of the forms, and so he cannot be the same as the forms.

## The receptacle

One of the so-called 'three kinds', the receptacle, is especially hard to understand, as Timaeus himself says. The incomprehensibility of the receptacle is inherent in its nature, so we should not expect much clarity; but a few notes might help us see the sort of difficulties it presents. The third kind, so-called, is first introduced in response to the question: what were the nature and qualities of the four bodies – air, water, fire and earth – before the creation of the cosmos? This question arose in turn because Timaeus pointed out that there was another principle, necessity, which attached to the nature of bodies as such, irrespective of the intelligent cause. The thought seems to be that in order to understand necessity, we need to understand the nature of the simple bodies, irrespective of the work they do for the good in the cosmos, and the best way of understanding this is to see what they were like before the world was ordered for the good, i.e. before the creation of the cosmos. However, the character of the simple bodies before the creation of the cosmos was in large part dependent on the receptacle. The nature of the dependence is a matter of dispute, however. There are two interpretations of the receptacle, which offer different notions of how bodies relate to the receptacle. One says that the receptacle is matter, where by 'matter' we should understand something like the stuff that bodies are made from. On the other interpretation, the receptacle is to be understood rather as that 'in which' bodies occur, that is, the place or space that bodies occupy. What divides the two interpretations is normally – though perhaps not correctly[4] – taken to be whether the receptacle enters into the composition of bodies or not: on the 'matter view' it does, on the 'space view' it does not. So, we might think, the space that a dog occupies is not a part of the dog, but its matter, its flesh and bones, is. The space interpretation seems to be on firm ground in that Timaeus repeatedly refers to the receptacle as 'space' (*chôra*) and as that 'in which' the appearances occur. Moreover, given that Timaeus is concerned to describe bodies as always changing, and conceives of change primarily in terms of spatial relocation, there is good reason for him to forefront the need for a spatial matrix. On the other hand, the expectation that bodies, particularly understood as geometrical solids, should somehow be constituted out of something material is not unreasonable. We may, for example, wonder how geometrical shapes that are not shapes of some sort of stuff could themselves end up constituting the concrete bodies that surround us.

A closely related question to the function of the receptacle is the character of the bodies. Timaeus characterizes them as fleeting appearances, which occur now here, now there in the receptacle. The situation, he says, is like that of a piece of gold constantly being shaped into new figures, where we cannot say that there is a triangle or a quadrangle in it because the shape is constantly changing (50a–c). Similarly, the appearances of the bodies have no substantiality; hence we cannot refer to them as being *this* or *that*, but we should refer to the receptacle as being 'such like' here and there depending on whether it is briefly qualified by fiery, watery, earthy, or airy appearances in different parts. One question that emerges here is whether Timaeus means to characterize the way bodies always are, both before and after the creation of the cosmos. Readers have often taken this to be Plato's own view of sensible bodies, referring sometimes also to a passage in the *Theaetetus* (156a–157c) where a view of sensibles as subject to extreme 'Heraclitean' flux is developed. Another option is that Timaeus means to characterize just the chaotic state of appearances before god ordered the bodies. The answer seems to be somewhere in

between: Timaeus is characterizing the way bodies are irrespective of the divine ordering. This applies especially to the state
of the bodies before the cosmos, but it also applies to the bodies
after their ordering, since it describes a tendency that bodies
still have as such. That after all was the point from which we
started: we wanted to know what contribution bodily necessity
*as such* made to the cosmos, independently of the intelligent
design. So it is quite appropriate that the description of the
bodies should be one that applies especially but not exclusively
to the pre-cosmos.

## Soul and body

We saw that the reason for god's creation of the world was his
desire to make another thing as good as possible and so like
himself. We also saw that god was essentially characterized by
intelligence. It should come as no surprise, therefore, that his
first creative act is to endow the cosmos with intelligence. However, for a visible, created thing, Timaeus says, having intelligence also implies having a soul, while having a soul in turn
implies having a body. The cosmos thus becomes an ensouled
body, qualifying as a living being. The account of the cosmic
soul and body occupies Timaeus up till 69, after which the
exposition turns to the composition of the human soul and
body, which is itself modelled on that of the cosmic soul and
body. One might say, therefore, that Timaeus' entire cosmology
is in fact biology.

The soul for Timaeus has priority over the body, as its principle and master. The soul is composed out of a mixture of
what Timaeus refers to as divisible and indivisible kinds of
Being, Sameness and Difference. The point of this obscure composition seems to be twofold.[5] First it must explain how the
world-soul can perform its cognitive functions. So cognition,
such as thinking, believing and perceiving, seems for Timaeus
to rely on making judgements as to whether something is the
same as or different from something else in the sphere either of
eternal being or of what comes into being. On the principle
that 'like is known by like', the soul is able to make judgements

about these factors because they are also elements of its constitution. The second reason for composing the world-soul the
way Timaeus does is to explain its ability to move. At 57d (ff.)
he says that unlikeness is responsible for motion and likeness
for rest. So we can see how he might think that mixing sameness
and difference with being would enable the world-soul to move
while also remaining unchanged in other respects. Just as the
mixture of the world-soul is meant to explain its basic ability
to move, so the way the mixture is organized is meant to explain
the way it moves. The mixture is mathematically structured
according to the harmonic scale, allowing for it to move in an
orderly and proportionate manner, and then divided and bent
to form eight circular hoops, seven of which correspond to the
motions of the planets.

The world body is so crafted as to accommodate the soul
that rules it. The body is spherical, as appropriate to the circular
motions of its soul. The soul covers the body from without and
extends throughout its inside. The motions of the world-soul
thus translate into that of the world body. However, the world
body itself is also composed at a basic level so as to display
good order. Fire and earth are employed to ensure the visibility
and tangibility of the body (without which we would not be
able to perceive it) and then air and water are introduced to
bind the other two in a proportionate relationship (31b–32c).
Indeed, the same principles of proportionality which god
invested in the world-soul are used in arranging the four
bodies.[6] At an even lower level of composition, the four bodies
are made of two sorts of triangle, which also combine according
to geometrical principles (53c–57c).[7] Being geometrically proportionate ensures that the bodies (with the exception of earth)
can change into each other (54b–c) and form larger compound
bodies. So both from the top down, through the motions of the
world-soul, and from the bottom up, through the proportionate
composition of its materials, the world body is crafted so as to
represent and promote the order of the cosmos.

The creation of mortal beings, first of all humans, has the
purpose of making the universe as complete as possible by
containing all the kinds of living being present in its paradigm.

The cosmic demiurge creates the immortal soul but hands over the job of making the mortal parts of the soul and the human body to the 'lesser gods', that is, the cosmic gods that he has created. Our immortal soul is created in the same way as the world-soul, albeit with less pure ingredients. The likeness between human and cosmic souls is of great ethical importance. When the soul is embodied it loses its rational shape because of the commotion of the body. This is how we come to be ruled at first by appetites and irrational desires. But because the soul is in origin rational, even when disturbed, it is able when properly educated to understand the rational motions of the world-soul. By understanding these motions it assimilates itself to them and thereby becomes orderly and temperate again (47b–c, 90c–d).[8] The similarity between the human and the world souls thus underwrites our ability to become better persons.

For Timaeus the four bodies move with linear motions, up and down, sideways, forwards and backwards. When the rational soul is first embodied it is affected by the linear motions of body. It thereby loses its natural circular shape and suffers all sorts of irrational confusion. Being affected by bodily motions is a matter of brute necessity. Given this necessity, however, the lesser gods have done their best to shape human nature so as to promote our rationality. As for the soul, they have divided it into the three parts familiar from the *Republic*, the rational, the spirited and the appetitive parts. The point of the division is twofold: it helps minimize the interference of the irrational affections in the deliberations of the ruling rational part, and it allows for parts dedicated to performing the functions required of a rational *embodied* being, such as eating, drinking, procreating, and defending oneself against inner and outer threats. The human body is also constructed so as to help us live embodied lives as rationally as possible. So the body has three distinct regions, head, heart and lower abdomen, which service the three parts of the soul. They are connected by the marrow which links the rational principle in the head through the trunk of the body down to the reproductive organs. Minor details show how god's provision extends beyond the life of the individual human being: so our nails have been created in a way that allows them to grow into the claws of the wild animals into whose shape some of us will be reborn (76d–e). One may regard the entire human body and soul as an integrated teleological system designed for the promotion of our good for the duration of our embodiment.

## The *Critias*: the foundation and fate of Atlantis

The aim of the story of Atlantis is to show the success of the virtuous city in action. The world, Timaeus has shown, is such as to sustain and promote goodness over irrationality both at the cosmic level and at the human level, if we so choose. Critias takes over citizens with Socrates' education and Timaeus' nature and shows how they prevail against what someone today might call 'the evil empire'. Atlantis is then, in a sense, a foil for the encomium of the ideal city. This is not to forget that Plato also has interests in Atlantis. However, it is important to understand the extent to which Atlantis is set up as a negative to ancient Athens; for herein lies the clue to understanding much of the Atlantis story.

Let us first consider the description of the foundation of Atlantis as compared to that of Athens. Both cities were founded by gods, but in contrasting circumstances. Athens was founded by the virgin Athena in order to produce men like herself, that is to say, philosopher-warriors (*Timaeus* 24c–d). Atlantis, in contrast, was founded by Poseidon as a way of protecting a young maid with whom he was having intercourse. In terms of the tripartite psychology, one could say that where Athens is a projection of the intellectual-spirited, Atlantis is already from its inception based on the appetitive.

The planning of the two cities is equally telling. The appetitive character of Atlantis is brought home through a range of details on which it contrasts with Athens. Athens was built in an area of exceptional fertility, the Attica of Critias' time being a mere 'skeleton' in comparison. The fertility of Attica is politically significant because it allows the warrior class of Athens the material means to focus on their profession, without also having to farm, so complying with the strict division of labour in the ideal city. The city itself was focused on the Acropolis. The different classes of citizen occupied separate parts, with the military class on top and the craftsmen and farmers on its slopes. They had no luxuries, no gold or silver, and drew water from a single spring. Contrast now Atlantis. Where landlocked Athens was self-sufficient because of the fertility of its soil and the frugality of its populace, the island of Atlantis received many imports to support its luxurious lifestyle. The sea not only surrounds it, it also enters it: the central island is surrounded by three concentric rings of water and two rings of earth, all connected by canals and bridges (see Figure 9 in *Critias* note 15). Given this network of waterways, every part is accessible from the sea, and so all of Atlantis counts, in a sense, as a harbour. As often in Plato, the sea represents exposure to the corruptive influence of money and luxuries. *Laws* 705d makes the point explicit: '[Being situated by the sea] fills the land with wholesaling and retailing, breeds shifty and deceitful habits in a man's soul, and makes the citizens distrustful and hostile, not only among themselves, but also in their dealings with the world outside' (transl. T. Saunders). Again, where Athens has no gold or silver, Atlantis possesses precious metals and alloys galore, including the outlandish 'orichalc'. Tellingly, Atlantis is home to the elephant, the 'largest and most voracious of beasts' (*Critias* 114e–115a). Where Athens is simple, Atlantis is a city of mixtures. So where Athens has one spring, Atlantis has two springs, a hot and cold. For visual pleasure its buildings are painted in a variety of colours and decorated with assorted metals. Everything about Atlantis reads like a case-study in *poikilia*, the variegation which in the *Republic* (557c) characterizes the irrational appetitive soul, and in the *Timaeus* the diseases of the body (82b). Indeed, the term variegated (*poikilos*) is itself used repeatedly (*Critias* 116b, 116d, 118b) to describe the material culture of Atlantis. The contrast with the simplicity and unity of the ideal city is implied.

The political constitution of ancient Athens we know: it is that of Socrates' ideal city. Atlantis, in contrast, is a dynasty of ten kings under the overall command of the House of Atlas.

The kings are free to lay down the law for their own subjects and to execute any of them at will. Only their behaviour towards each other is regulated, by a written law going back to Poseidon. They pledge their allegiance to the law by slaughtering a bull and washing the lettering with its blood. There is much here that is reminiscent of Asian tyrannies. However, part of the material for the description of Atlantis also comes from fifth-century democratic Athens.[9] This is not as much of a contradiction as we might think since, for Plato, tyranny is the natural development of democracy (cf. *Republic* 571a ff.), both being political externalizations of the disorderly appetitive soul.

This is not to ignore that Atlantis has blessings that give it the *appearance* of a utopia. At first the Atlantids certainly appeared to be virtuous because of the divine element they had inherited from their founder. As the divine element dwindled, however, their ability to withstand the corrupting influence of their wealth weakened. As we know from the *Republic*, even the best constitution decays, despite its measures to prevent change. *A fortiori* a society that lacks the rule of reason will end up being controlled by its appetites. The material blessings of Atlantis are then from the point of view of true politics a smoke-screen. One might even say that part of the evil of Atlantis lies in its deceptive attractiveness, like the lifestyle of a tyrant. If Atlantis looks like a utopia to us, we should recall that it is an *appetitive* utopia, and so, in Plato's eyes, a *dystopia*. Whether we are attracted to ancient Athens or Atlantis may indeed serve as a test of our own grasp of the real good (cf. *Critias* 121b).

I have been at pains to point out the ways in which Atlantis is deliberately *set up* to contrast with Athens, as a sort of negative to the ideal city. Those who are tempted to read the Atlantis story as a historical document need to bear in mind the extent to which it has been constructed by Plato to suit his own philosophical purposes. We cannot understand Atlantis other than in the context of Plato's own political recommendations. What about the great disaster, it may be asked? Is this not a reminiscence of some actual historical event? Of course

there have been many historical disasters which Plato might
have had in mind. The volcanic eruption at Thera (Santorini)
which devastated parts of the Aegean in the fifteenth century
BC is one such event.[10] However, more important for the purposes of understanding the Atlantis story is the view shared by
Plato and other ancient philosophers (Heraclitus, Aristotle, the
Stoics, to name some) according to which the world (bar Egypt,
perhaps) is subject to cyclical physical disasters which regularly
set the clock of human history back to Year Zero. The disaster
that wiped out Atlantis and Athens is really just one of numerous which periodically recur because of certain planetary
motions (*Timaeus* 22d–23b).[11] The point for Plato, then, is not
the occurrence of any particular historical event, but rather the
validity of a general view of the cosmos.

## The end of the *Critias*

The *Critias* ends at the point when Zeus is about to announce
his punishment of Atlantis. The work therefore seems incomplete. Various explanations have been offered. One theory is
that the work is deliberately left incomplete, perhaps as a reflection of Critias' limited abilities or devious character.[12] It should
be noted, however, that Critias says (*Timaeus* 26c) that he
has already delivered his speech to his companions the same
morning; so it seems that the feat of completing the speech is
not beyond him. Another suggestion is that Plato abandoned
the project because he thought that the story could be told
better in the context of the *Laws*, where in Book III we are
told of the near destruction of civilization by a deluge and its
subsequent history down to Plato's day. This suggestion also
gives us an idea for what Hermocrates might have spoken
about, namely, the account of the different kinds of constitution
now also contained in the *Laws*.[13] One worry with this suggestion, however, is that it makes the scope of Plato's project far
exceed what is announced by Critias as the speakers' brief.
There is no indication that the speakers are interested in bringing the account down to historical times. A final option is that
Plato abandoned the *Critias* because he realized that spelling

out the Atlantis story was, in a way, superfluous: given Timaeus'
account of cosmic justice and punishment through reincar-
nation of wicked souls, we know the sort of punishment that
lies in store for the Atlantids. This would explain the point at
which it is abandoned, when Zeus is about to announce his
punishment. There is no longer a need to spell out the details
of a particular dispensation of divine justice, given our understanding of cosmic justice in general.

## The translation

As the translation is in essence and most detail Sir Desmond
Lee's, his words on the style should be allowed to stand. At the
end I add a note of explanation on the revisions I have made.
Lee wrote:

> The two dialogues have particular difficulties for the translator.
> The Greek is by common consent difficult. In the *Timaeus* in
> particular Plato is dealing with an unfamiliar subject – nowhere
> else does he deal at length with the origin or nature of the physical
> world; he is telling a creation story, which leads in places to the
> use of more elevated language than a more ordinary theme. And
> these factors may account for some of the peculiar difficulties of
> the language which he uses. But Plato's style also changed as he
> grew older. The changes include not only unconscious tricks of
> usage, which because they are unconscious are invaluable to
> stylometry in its attempt to order the dialogues chronologically;
> they also include a number of conscious devices, like avoid-
> ance of hiatus[14] and deliberate adjustment of word order, which
> make for less easy reading. Add to this a certain stiffness, a lack
> of ease and vitality that characterized the earlier dialogues, and
> you have in brief the main characteristics of the original Greek:
> elaborate, often deliberately contrived, dealing with unfamiliar
> material for which no ready vocabulary existed, sometimes
> solemn, and lacking in the lively clarity and natural vigour of
> earlier work.
>
> Faced with these difficulties the translator's first duty is to
> make out the meaning as clearly as he can with the aid of the

commentators. He must then decide how far he should try to reproduce the characteristics of the original in his English version. Of the two most recent translators,[15] Taylor tries to catch the solemnity of the original by a certain archaism. But Plato did not seem archaic when he wrote, and archaism conveys a wrong atmosphere and does not make for clear understanding. Cornford is direct and full, concerned that the reader shall have in English all the detail of what Plato said; and there is his commentary to explain, add, or subtract. For a reader without a commentary, what Plato meant is as important as what he said, and the full detail of a literal rendering can not only seem unnatural in English but also make understanding more difficult. No attempt has therefore been made here to reproduce the peculiar character of the Greek; the object has been to discover Plato's meaning and express it in the sort of English we actually use. Something is thereby lost, and at times the complications of the Greek may distort the English. But it seems the best way to serve the modern reader, and even in plain language something of the grandeur of Plato's thought may be apparent.

*

The translation has been made from Burnet's text in the Oxford Classical Texts,[16] with a note of any variations adopted. The two main modern commentaries in English on the *Timaeus* are Taylor's *A Commentary on Plato's Timaeus*, and Cornford's *Plato's Cosmology*. I have used these constantly and my debt to them will be apparent; especially my debt to Cornford, whose work is the later of the two and whose lectures on the *Timaeus* I once attended.

The virtue of Lee's translation is its readability. He achieved this by frequently compressing and refiguring Plato's Greek. The price was, at times, a lack of precision and correspondence with the Greek. The present edition is a revision and not a retranslation, so I have not generally attempted to change the character of Lee's rendition. However, I have tried to inject greater accuracy than Lee thought necessary in passages of particular interpretative importance. There are other translations on the market that are more precise in the sense of more literal. The aim of this revision is to serve the reader who, while feeling no need to experience every bump in the road, still wants to track significant details in Plato's text. Also, as part of the revision, several notes have been removed and others added, to which I have attached my initials (TJ).

## Notes

1. See D. Sedley, *Creationism and Its Critics in Antiquity*, chs. 1–2, for an illuminating account of intelligent-design theories in pre-Platonic thought.

2. Cf. G. R. Carone, *Plato's Cosmology and Its Ethical Dimensions*, p. 49.

3. Aristotle, *De Caelo* 280a1.

4. Cf. V. Harte, *Plato on Parts and Wholes*, pp. 247–64, in particular pp. 250–51.

5. Cf. Aristotle, *De Anima* 406b28–31, and D. Frede, 'The Philosophical Economy of Plato's Psychology: Rationality and Common Concepts in the *Timaeus*', in M. Frede and G. Striker (eds.), *Rationality in Greek Thought*, pp. 29–58.

6. Cf. F. M. Cornford, *Plato's Cosmology*, p. 49.

7. For a full account, see G. Vlastos, *Plato's Universe*, pp. 66–97.

8. Cf. D. Sedley, 'The Ideal of Godlikeness', in G. Fine (ed.), *Plato. Oxford Readings in Philosophy*, pp. 791–810.

9. See P. Vidal-Naquet, 'Athènes et l'Atlantide', in *Le Chasseur noir: formes de pensée et formes de société dans le monde grec*, pp. 335–60.

10. See, e.g., J. V. Luce, *The End of Atlantis*. For judicious discussion of Luce and other 'factual accounts', see C. Gill (ed.), *Plato: The Atlantis Story*, pp. viii–xii.

11. Note that Atlantis and Athens are both destroyed in the same round of catastrophes (25c–d), so the punishment of Atlantis is not explained simply by its obliteration.

12. Cf. W. Welliver, *Character, Plot and Thought in Plato's Timaeus-Critias*, p. 44.

13. Cf. Cornford, *Plato's Cosmology*, pp. 7–8; on the relationship between the Atlantis story and the *Laws*, see also C. Gill, 'Plato and Politics: The *Critias* and the *Politicus*', *Phronesis* 24, pp. 148–67.

14. The occurrence of two vowel sounds next to each other, typically

at the end of one word and the beginning of the next, without
an intermediate consonant sound. (TJ)

15. 'Recent' in 1965. (TJ)
16. J. Burnet (ed.), *Platonis Opera*, vol. IV (Oxford, 1902). (TJ)

# Further Reading

## Translations and commentaries

Archer-Hind, R. D. (ed. and tr.), *The Timaeus of Plato* (London, 1888; reprinted Salem, NH, 1988)

Bury, R. G. (ed. and tr.), *Plato: Timaeus, Critias, Cleitophon, Menexenus, Epistles* (Cambridge, MA, 1960)

Cornford, F. M., *Plato's Cosmology* (London, 1937; reprinted Indianapolis, 1997)

Gill, C. (ed.), *Plato: The Atlantis Story* (Bristol, 1980)

Taylor, A. E., *A Commentary on Plato's 'Timaeus'* (Oxford, 1928; reprinted New York, 1967)

Zeyl, D. J. (tr.), *Plato: Timaeus* (Indianapolis, 2000)

## On the relationship of the *Timaeus* to Presocratic philosophy

Naddaf, G., 'Plato and the *Peri Phuseôs* tradition', in T. Calvo and L. Brisson (eds.), *Interpreting the Timaeus-Critias* (Sankt Augustin, 1997), pp. 27–37

Sedley, D., *Creationism and Its Critics in Antiquity* (Berkeley, 2007)

## On the place of the *Timaeus-Critias* in Plato's later work

Cherniss, H., 'The Relation of the *Timaeus* to Plato's Later Dialogues', *American Journal of Philology* 78 (1957), pp. 225–66; also in his *Selected Papers*, L. Tarán (ed.) (Leiden, 1977), pp. 298–339

Gill, C., 'Plato and Politics: The *Critias* and the *Politicus*', *Phronesis* 24 (1979), pp. 148–67

Owen, G. E. L., 'The Place of the *Timaeus* in Plato's Dialogues', in R. E. Allen (ed.), *Studies in Plato's Metaphysics* (London and New York, 1965), pp. 313–38, and in G. E. L. Owen, *Logic, Science and Dialectic*, M. C. Nussbaum (ed.) (Ithaca, 1986), pp. 65–84

## On Aristotle's relationship to the *Timaeus*

Cherniss, H., *Aristotle's Criticism of Plato and the Academy*, vol. 1 (Baltimore, 1944)

Sedley, *Creationism and Its Critics in Antiquity*, ch. 5

## On the contribution of the *Timaeus* to the history of science

Gregory, A., *Plato's Philosophy of Science* (London, 2000)

Sambursky, S., *The Physical World of the Greeks* (London, 1963)

Vlastos, G., *Plato's Universe* (Seattle, 1975)

## On the Atlantis story, its status as history or otherwise, and its function within Plato's political philosophy and the role of Critias

Brisson, L., *Plato, the Myth Maker* (Chicago, 1998)

Broadie, S., 'Theodicy and Pseudo-History in the *Timaeus*', *Oxford Studies in Ancient Philosophy* 21 (2001), pp. 1–28

Gill, C., 'Plato's Atlantis Story and the Birth of Fiction', *Philosophy and Literature* 3 (1979), pp. 64–78

—, 'The Genre of the Atlantis Story', *Classical Philology* 72 (1977), pp. 287–304

Johansen, T. K., *Plato's Natural Philosophy* (Cambridge, 2004), ch. 2

Luce, J. V., *The End of Atlantis* (London, 1969)

Morgan, K. A., 'Designer History: Plato's Atlantis Story and

Fourth-Century Ideology', *Journal of Hellenic Studies* 118 (1998), pp. 101–18

Pradeau, J.-F., *Le Monde de la Politique* (Sankt Augustin, 1997)

Rowe, C. J., 'The Status of the "Myth"', in C. Natali and S. Maso (eds.), *Plato Physicus* (Amsterdam, 2003), pp. 21–31

Vidal-Naquet, P., 'Athènes et l'Atlantide', in *Le Chasseur noir: formes de pensée et formes de société dans le monde grec* (Paris, 1981), pp. 335–60; English translation by A. Szegedy-Maszak, *The Black Hunter: Forms of Thought and Forms of Society in the Greek World* (Baltimore, 1986)

Welliver, W., *Character, Plot and Thought in Plato's Timaeus-Critias* (Leiden, 1977)

## On the status of the *Timaeus*' cosmology as likely 'myth'

Burnyeat, M. F., 'ΕΙΚΩΣ ΜΥΘΟΣ', *Rhizai*, vol. 2, no. 2 (2005), pp. 143–66

Johansen, *Plato's Natural Philosophy*, ch. 3

Tarán, L., 'The Creation Myth in Plato's *Timaeus*', in J. P. Anton and G. Kustas (eds.), *Essays in Ancient Greek Philosophy*, vol. 1 (Albany, 1971), pp. 372–407

Vlastos, G., 'Creation in the *Timaeus*: is it a fiction?', in Allen (ed.), *Studies in Plato's Metaphysics*, pp. 401–19

## On teleology in the *Timaeus-Critias*

Johansen, *Plato's Natural Philosophy*, ch. 4

Lennox, J., 'Plato's Unnatural Teleology', in J. Lennox, *Aristotle's Philosophy of Biology: Studies in the Origins of Life Science* (Cambridge, 2001), pp. 280–302

Mueller, I., 'Platonism and the Study of Nature (Phaedo 95eff.)', in J. Gentzler (ed.), *Method in Ancient Philosophy* (Oxford, 1988), pp. 67–90

Sedley, *Creationism and Its Critics in Antiquity*, ch. 4

## On the ethical aspects of cosmology

Carone, G. R., *Plato's Cosmology and Its Ethical Dimensions* (Cambridge, 2005)

Sedley, D., ' "Becoming like god" in the *Timaeus* and Aristotle', in Calvo and Brisson (eds.), *Interpreting the Timaeus-Critias*, pp. 327–40; reprinted in revised form as 'The Ideal of God-likeness', in G. Fine (ed.), *Plato. Oxford Readings in Philosophy* (Oxford, 2000), pp. 791–810

## For the interpretation of god in the *Timaeus* and other Platonic works

Hackforth, R., 'Plato's Theism', in Allen (ed.), *Studies in Plato's Metaphysics*, pp. 439–47

Menn, S., *Plato on God as Nous* (Carbondale, 1995)

Mohr, R., *The Platonic Cosmology* (Leiden, 1985); new, expanded edition, *God and Forms in Plato* (Las Vegas, 2005)

## For analysis of the composition of bodies and the role of the receptacle

Cherniss, H., 'A Much Misread Passage of the *Timaeus* (*Timaeus* 49c7–50b5)', *American Journal of Philology* 75 (1954), pp. 113–30

Gill, M. L., 'Matter and Flux in Plato's *Timaeus*', *Phronesis* 32 (1987), pp. 34–53

Harte, V., *Plato on Parts and Wholes* (Oxford, 2002)

Miller, D., *The Third Kind in Plato's Timaeus* (Göttingen, 2003)

Silverman, A., 'Timaean Particulars', *Classical Quarterly* NS 42 (1992), pp. 87–113

## On the role of 'necessity' in cosmology

Johansen, *Plato's Natural Philosophy*, ch. 5

Mason, A. S., 'Plato on Necessity and Chaos', *Philosophical Studies* 127 (2006), pp. 283–98

Morrow, G., 'Necessity and Persuasion in Plato's *Timaeus*', in Allen (ed.), *Studies in Plato's Metaphysics*, pp. 421–37

Strange, S. K., 'The Double Explanation in the *Timaeus*', in G. Fine (ed.), *Plato 1: Metaphysics and Epistemology* (Oxford, 1999), pp. 397–415

## For accounts of the theory of motion in the *Timaeus*

Karfik, F., *Die Beseelung des Kosmos* (Leipzig, 2004)

Lee, E. N., 'Reason and Rotation: Circular Movement as the Model of Mind (*Nous*) in the Later Plato', in W. H. Werkmeister (ed.), *Facets of Plato's Philosophy* (Assen, 1976), pp. 70–102

Skemp, J. B., *The Theory of Motion in Plato's Later Dialogues* (Cambridge, 1942)

Vlastos, G., 'The Disorderly Motion in the *Timaeus*', in Allen (ed.), *Studies in Plato's Metaphysics*, pp. 379–99

## On the composition of the soul

Frede, D., 'The Philosophical Economy of Plato's Psychology: Rationality and Common Concepts in the *Timaeus*', in M. Frede and G. Striker (eds.), *Rationality in Greek Thought* (Oxford, 1996), pp. 29–58

Johansen, *Plato's Natural Philosophy*, ch. 7

## On the role of mathematics in the *Timaeus*

Burnyeat, M. F., 'Plato on Why Mathematics is Good for the Soul', in T. Smiley (ed.), *Mathematics and Necessity: Essays in the History of Philosophy*, Proceedings of the British Academy 103 (Oxford, 1999), pp. 1–81

Lloyd, G. E. R., 'Plato on Mathematics and Nature, Myth and Science', in G. E. R. Lloyd, *Methods and Problems in Greek Science* (Cambridge, 1991), pp. 333–51

## On the argument for the uniqueness of the world, *Timaeus* 31a–b

Keyt, D., 'The Mad Craftsman of the *Timaeus*', *Philosophical Review* 80 (1971), pp. 230–35; with reply by Burnyeat, 'ΕΙΚΩΣ ΜΥΘΟΣ', pp. 160–61

## On the narrative form of the *Timaeus*

Johansen, *Plato's Natural Philosophy*, ch. 9
Osborne, C., 'Space, Time, Shape, and Direction: Creative Discourse in the *Timaeus*', in C. Gill and M. M. McCabe (eds.), *Form and Argument in Late Plato* (Oxford, 1996), pp. 179–211

## Collections of articles on various themes in the *Timaeus-Critias*

Calvo, T., and Brisson, L. (eds.), *Interpreting the Timaeus-Critias* (Sankt Augustin, 1997)
Reydams-Schils, G. (ed.), *Plato's Timaeus as Cultural Icon* (Notre Dame, 2003)
Wright, M. R. (ed.), *Reason and Necessity: Essays on Plato's Timaeus* (London and Swansea, 2000)

# TIMAEUS

# Summary of contents of the *Timaeus* by numbered sections

### Main section III.
### *Reason and necessity working together*

# Characters in the Dialogue

SOCRATES

TIMAEUS of Locri, in Southern Italy. There is no evidence for his historical existence, but he may have been modelled on Archytas of Tarentum, philosopher and statesman, whom Plato met on his first visit to Sicily (*c.* 388 BC).

CRITIAS of Athens. He may be one of several relatives of Plato. Chronologically, he is more likely to be Plato's maternal great grandfather; however, scholars have also identified him with Plato's mother's cousin Critias, a poet and a member of the so-called Thirty, who presided over a rule of terror in Athens in 404–403 BC.[1]

HERMOCRATES of Syracuse. Statesman and soldier, who took a prominent part in the defeat of the Athenian expedition against Sicily (413–410 BC).

The dramatic date of the dialogue is *c.* 425 BC, when Socrates was about forty-five.

*It is customary to refer to Plato's works by reference to the page of an early edition, that of Stephanus, 1578. These numbers, divided into equal sections a, b, c, d and e, are printed in the margin of the translation.*

*The headings and figures were introduced by Desmond Lee as an aid to the reader; they are not part of Plato's text.*

1. *Introductory conversation (a). Socrates has, on the previous day, described an ideal city, like that outlined in Plato's* Republic. *He would like an account of his citizens in action, which he calls on the others to provide.*

SOCRATES: One, two, three – but where, my dear Timaeus, is the fourth of my guests of yesterday who were to entertain me today?  17a

TIMAEUS: He's fallen sick, Socrates; otherwise he would never willingly have missed today's discussion.

SOCRATES: Then if he's away it is up to you and the others here to fulfil his part as well as your own.

TIMAEUS: Yes; we'll certainly do our best. For it wouldn't  b be just, after the faultless hospitality you showed your guests yesterday, if the rest of us were not eager to entertain you in return.

SOCRATES: Do you remember, then, the subjects I set you and their scope?

TIMAEUS: Some of them; and you are here to remind us of any we have forgotten. Better still, if it's not too much trouble, give us a brief summary of the discussion, to fortify our memory.

SOCRATES: I will. Yesterday my main object, I suppose, was  c to describe my view of the best constitution and its citizens.

TIMAEUS: And we all very much liked the city which you described, Socrates.

SOCRATES: We began, did we not, by separating the class of farmers and the other crafts from that of the defence forces?

TIMAEUS: Yes.

SOCRATES: And we assigned to each class, as being natural
d  to it, a single appropriate occupation or craft. So those whose
   duty it was to fight on behalf of all would be the city's sole
18a guards against threat of harm, whether external or internal:
   they would be gentle in administering justice to their subjects,
   who were their natural friends, and tough in fighting battles
   against external enemies.

TIMAEUS: Certainly.

SOCRATES: And to ensure the appropriate gentleness and
toughness in their behaviour to each, we said, I think, that the
nature of the guards' soul must combine the spirited and the
philosophical to a rare degree.

TIMAEUS: Yes.

SOCRATES: As for their nurture, they were to be trained in
physical exercise, the arts, and in all the studies appropriate to
them.

TIMAEUS: Of course.

b  SOCRATES: Having been so brought up, they must never, I
   think we said, regard gold or silver or anything else as their own
   private property, but earn a wage like mercenaries, sufficient for
   their moderate needs, in return for the safeguard they afforded
   to those under their protection. They were to share all expendi-
   ture and live a common life together, devoting their attention
   wholly to excellence, freed from all other preoccupations.

TIMAEUS: That was what we said.

c  SOCRATES: And we had something to say about the women,
   too. Their natures were to be moulded similarly to men's, and
   they were all to share the same occupations both in war and in
   the rest of life.

TIMAEUS: We said that too.

SOCRATES: I expect you remember what was said about the
production of children, because it was unusual. We laid it down
that marriages and children should be shared in common by
all, and arranged that no one should recognize any child born
as their own, but that all should regard themselves as related
d  to everyone else. So all those born within the appropriate period
   would regard each other as brothers and sisters, anyone born

earlier than themselves as parents and grandparents, and anyone born later than themselves as children and grandchildren.

TIMAEUS: Yes, the provisions you describe are easy to
remember.

SOCRATES: And to ensure that their natures should from the
start be the best possible, you will remember that we said that
the male and female rulers should secretly arrange the lots so   e
that bad and good men are separated and allocated for mating
to women like themselves, and prevent any possible consequent
ill-feeling by letting it be supposed that the allocation was due
to chance.

TIMAEUS: I remember.

SOCRATES: You will remember too that we said that the   19a
children of the good were to be brought up and cared for, and
those of the bad distributed secretly among the rest of the
community; and the rulers were to keep a constant eye on the
children as they grew up and promote in turn any who deserved
it, and degrade into the places of the promoted any in their
own ranks who seemed unworthy of their position.

TIMAEUS: So we said.

SOCRATES: Is that an adequate summary of yesterday's discussion, my dear Timaeus, or has anything been left out that
we miss?

TIMAEUS: There is nothing, Socrates; these were the things   b
that were said.

SOCRATES: Let me now go on to tell you how I feel about
the constitution we have described. My feelings are rather like
those of a man who has somewhere seen some splendid animals,
either in a picture or really alive but motionless, and wants to
see them moving and competing for prizes in an activity which
seems appropriate to their physiques. That's exactly what I feel   c
about the city we have described. I would be glad to hear
someone give an account of it fighting with other cities in the
contests in which cities compete, entering a war in an appropriate way and showing in the fighting all the qualities one would
expect from its system of education and training, both in deeds
through its actions and in words by its negotiations with its
rivals.

d    Now, my dear Critias and Hermocrates, my own verdict on myself is that I shall never be able to praise the men and the city sufficiently. This, as far as I am concerned, is not surprising; but in my opinion the same is true of the poets, past and present. Not that I have a low opinion of the tribe of poets, but it is clear to all that the imitative people imitate best and most easily what they were brought up with, while what lies outside that experience is difficult to imitate well in deeds and even more so

e in words. The tribe of sophists, again, I have always thought to be quite experienced at making many and beautiful speeches on other subjects, but I am afraid that, because they wander from city to city and never manage a home of their own, they may fail to hit upon the sort of things that men who are at once philosophers and statesmen would do and say in war and in battles when they engage with enemies in action or in verbal conversations. There remains the tribe which is of your disposition, who is by nature and upbringing imbued with philos-

20a ophy and statesmanship. For Timaeus here comes from the well-ordered city of Locris in Italy, where he is second to none in wealth and birth: there he has enjoyed the highest offices and distinctions the city can offer, and has also in my opinion reached the highest eminence in every kind of philosophy. Critias I suppose all of us here know to be no amateur in these matters, while there are many witnesses to assure us that Hermocrates is qualified in them also, both by his natural gifts

b and by his education. I had this in mind yesterday when I agreed so readily to your request for an account of the constitution: I knew that there was no one more fitted to provide the sequel to it than you, if you were willing; for you are the only living people who could adequately describe my city fighting a war worthy of her. So when I had done what was asked of me, I set you the task I have just described. You agreed to put your heads

c together, and return today my hospitality by way of speeches; and here I am dressed in my best and looking forward to what I am about to receive.

2. *Introductory conversation (b). The Atlantis Myth;*
*the ideal city existed once in ancient Athens. The reply*
*to Socrates will comprise a cosmological account by*
*Timaeus, followed by an account of the struggle*
*between Atlantis and ancient Athens by Critias.*

HERMOCRATES: I assure you, Socrates, that, as Timaeus here
said, there will be no lack of willingness on our part and we
don't want to excuse ourselves from our part of the bargain.
Indeed, we were considering it as soon as we got back yesterday
to Critias' house, where we are staying, and even before that
while we were on the way there. Critias then produced an    d
account he had heard long ago. Tell it again now to Socrates,
Critias, so that we can see whether it is suitable for our purposes
or not.

CRITIAS: I will, if the other member of the trio, Timaeus,
agrees.

TIMAEUS: I agree.

CRITIAS: Listen then, Socrates. The account is a very strange
one, but Solon, the wisest of the seven wise men, once vouched    e
its complete truth. He was a relation and close friend of
Dropides, my great-grandfather, as he often says himself in his
poems, and told the story to my grandfather Critias, who in
turn repeated it to us when he was an old man. It relates the
many marvellous achievements of our city long ago, which have
been lost sight of because of the lapse of time and destruction
of human life. Of these the greatest is one that we could well    21a
recall now to repay our debt to you and to offer the Goddess
on her festival day² a just and truthful hymn of praise.

SOCRATES: Good. And what is this unrecorded yet authentic
achievement of our city in ancient times that Critias heard from
Solon and recounted to you?

CRITIAS: I will tell you; though the story was old when I
heard it and the man who told it to me was no longer young.
For Critias was at the time, so he said, nearly ninety, and I was    b
about ten. It was Children's Day in the festival of Apatouria,³
and there were the customary ceremonies for the boys, including prizes given by the fathers for reciting. There were

recitations of many poems by different authors, but many of
the competitors chose Solon's poems, which were in those days
quite a novelty. And one of the clansmen, either because he
c thought so or out of politeness to Critias, said that he thought
that Solon was not only the wisest of men but also the most
free-spirited of poets. And the old man – I remember it well –
was extremely pleased, and said with a smile, 'I wish, Amynander, that he hadn't treated poetry as a spare-time occupation
but had taken it seriously like others; if he had finished the
account he brought back from Egypt, and hadn't been com-
pelled to neglect it because of the uprisings and other evils he
d found here on his return, I don't think any poet, even Homer
or Hesiod, would have been held in higher esteem.' 'And what
was the account, Critias?' asked Amynander. 'It was about
what may fairly be called the greatest and most noteworthy of
all this city's achievements, but because of the lapse of time and
the death of those who took part in it the account has not lasted
till our day.' 'Tell us from the beginning,' came the reply; 'what
was it that Solon was saying and how and from whom had he
heard the account as true?'

e         'There is in Egypt,' said Critias, 'at the head of the delta,
where the Nile divides, a district called the Saïtic. The chief city
of the district, from which King Amasis came, is called Saïs.
The chief goddess of the inhabitants is called in Egyptian Neïth,
in Greek (according to them) Athena; and they are very friendly
to the Athenians and claim some relationship to them. Solon
said that he came there on his travels and was highly honoured
22a by them, and in the course of making inquiries about antiquity
from those priests who were most experienced in these things
found that both he and all his countrymen were almost entirely
ignorant about such matters. And wishing to lead them on to
talk about early times, he embarked on an account of the
earliest events known here, telling them the myths about Pho-
b roneus, said to be the first man, and Niobe, and how Deucalion
and Pyrrha survived the flood and who were their descendants,
and he reckoned up the generations after them, and tried to
calculate how long ago the events in question had taken place.
And a very old priest said to him, "Solon, Solon, you Greeks

are ever children; there is no such thing as an old Greek."
"What do you mean by that?" inquired Solon. "You are all
young in mind," came the reply: "you have in your minds no
belief rooted in old tradition and no knowledge hoary with age.
And the reason is this. There have been and will be many   c
different calamities to destroy mankind, the greatest of them
by fire and water, lesser ones by countless other causes. Your
own story of how Phaëthon, child of the sun, once harnessed
his father's chariot, but was unable to guide it along his father's
course and so burnt up things on the earth and was himself
destroyed by a thunderbolt, this story has the form of a myth,
but the truth is that there is at long intervals a variation in the   d
course of the heavenly bodies as they travel around the earth
and a consequent widespread destruction by fire of things on
the earth. On such occasions those who live in the mountains
or in high and dry places suffer more than those living by rivers
or by the sea; as for us, the Nile, our own regular saviour, is
freed to preserve us in this emergency. When on the other hand
the gods purge the earth with a deluge, the herdsmen and
shepherds in the mountains escape, but those living in the cities
in your part of the world are swept into the sea by the rivers;   e
here water never falls on the land from above either then or at
any other time, but rises up naturally from below. This is the
reason why our traditions here are said to be the oldest preserved; though the truth is that in all places where excessive
cold or heat does not prevent it human beings are always to be
found in larger or smaller numbers. But in our temples we have   23a
preserved from earliest times a written record of any great or
splendid achievement or notable event which has come to our
ears whether it occurred in your part of the world or here or
anywhere else; whereas with you and the others, writing and
the other necessities of cities have only just been developed
when, after the usual number of years, the heavenly flood
descends on you like a disease, and spares none but the unlet-
tered and uncultured, so that again you come into being from   b
the beginning like children, in complete ignorance of what
happened in our part of the world or in yours in early times.
So these genealogies of your own people which you were just

recounting, Solon, are little more than children's myths. You
remember only one deluge, though there have been many, and
you do not know that the finest and best race of men that ever
existed lived in your country; you and your fellow citizens are
c   descended from the little seed that remained, but you know
nothing about it because so many succeeding generations left
no record in writing. For before the greatest of all destructions
by water, Solon, the city that is now Athens was pre-eminent
in war and conspicuously the best governed in every way: its
achievements and constitution are said to have been the finest
of any in the world of which we have heard tell."

d       'Solon said that he was astonished at what he heard and
eagerly begged the priests to describe to him in detail the doings
of these citizens of the past. "I will gladly do so, Solon," replied
the priest, "both for your sake and your city's, but chiefly in
gratitude to the Goddess to whom it has fallen to bring up and
educate both your country and ours – yours first, when she
e   took over the seed from Earth and Hephaestus, ours a thousand
years later. The age of our political ordering is given in our
sacred records as eight thousand years, and the citizens whose
laws and whose finest achievement I will now briefly describe
24a  to you therefore lived nine thousand years ago; we will go
through their history in detail later on at leisure, when we can
consult the records.

'"Consider their laws compared with ours; for you will find
today among us many parallels to your institutions in those
days. First, our priestly class is kept distinct from the others;
next, as for the class of craftsmen, you will find that each class
– shepherds, hunters, farmers – by itself performs its function
b   without mingling with any of the others. And of course you
will have noticed that our warrior class is kept separate from
all others, being forbidden by the law to undertake any duties
other than military: moreover their armament consists of shield
and spear, which we were the first people in Asia[4] to adopt,
under the instruction of the Goddess, as you were in your part
of the world. And again you see, I trust, what great attention
our law devotes to wisdom, right from its principles: in the
study of the cosmos, it has traced all our knowledge from these

divine beings down to human affairs, including divination and   c
health-giving medicine, and it has acquired all other related
branches of knowledge. The Goddess founded this whole order
and system when she framed your society. She chose the place
in which you were born with an eye to its temperate climate,
which would produce men of high intelligence; for being herself
a lover of war and wisdom she picked a place for her first   d
foundation that would produce men most like herself in character. So you lived there under the laws I have described, and
even better ones, and excelled all men in every kind of accom-
plishment, as one would expect of children and offspring of the
gods. And among all the wonderful achievements recorded here
of your city, one stands out for its magnitude and its excellence.   e
Our records tell how your city checked a great power which
arrogantly advanced from its base in the Atlantic ocean to
attack the cities of Europe and Asia. For in those days the
Atlantic was navigable. There was an island opposite the strait
which you call (so you say) the Pillars of Heracles,[5] an island
larger than Libya and Asia combined; from it travellers could
in those days reach the other islands, and from them the whole   25a
opposite continent which surrounds what can truly be called
'the ocean'. For the sea within the strait we were talking about
is like a lake with a narrow entrance; the other ocean is the real
ocean and the land which entirely surrounds it is properly
termed 'continent'. On this island of Atlantis had arisen a
powerful and remarkable dynasty of kings, which ruled the
whole island, and many other islands as well and parts of the
continent; in addition it controlled, within the strait, Libya up   b
to the borders of Egypt and Europe as far as Tyrrhenia.[6] This
dynasty, gathering its whole power together, attempted to
enslave, at a single stroke, your country and ours and all the
territory within the strait. It was then, Solon, that the power of
your city became clear for all men to see in its excellence and
might. Her bravery and military skill were outstanding; she led
an alliance of the Greeks, and then when they deserted her and   c
she was forced to fight alone, after running into direst peril, she
overcame the invaders and celebrated a victory; she rescued
those not yet enslaved from the slavery threatening them,

and she generously freed all others living within the Pillars of
Heracles. At a later time there were earthquakes and floods of
d  extraordinary violence, and in a single dreadful day and night
all your fighting men were swallowed up by the earth, and the
island of Atlantis was similarly swallowed up by the sea and
vanished; this is why the sea in that area is to this day impassable
to navigation, which is hindered by mud just below the surface,
the remains of the sunken island.""'

You have heard in brief, Socrates, the story which Critias
e  told when he was an old man, and which he had heard from
Solon. While you were talking yesterday about the constitution
and the men you were describing, I was reminded of this story
and noticed with astonishment how closely, by some miracu-
lous stroke of luck, with no intention, your account coincided
26a  with Solon's. I was not willing to speak at once, for after so
long a time my recollection was imperfect; I decided therefore
that I must first rehearse the whole story to myself before telling
it. That was why I was so quick to agree to your conditions
yesterday, thinking that I was pretty well placed to deal with
what is always the most serious difficulty in such matters, how
to submit an account that suits one's purposes. And so, as
b  Hermocrates said, as soon as we left here yesterday I started
telling the story to the others as I remembered it, and when I
got back I managed to recall pretty well all of it by thinking it
over at night. It is amazing, as is often said, how what we learn
as children sticks in the memory. I'm not at all sure whether I
could remember again all I heard yesterday; yet I should be
surprised if any detail of this story I heard so long ago has
c  escaped me. I listened to it then with a child's intense delight,
and the old man was glad to answer my innumerable questions,
so that the details have been indelibly branded on my memory.
What is more, I have told the whole story to the others early
this morning, so that they might be as well placed as I am for
the day's speeches.

And now, to come to the point, I am ready to tell the story,
d  Socrates, not only in outline but in detail, as I heard it. We will
transfer to reality the citizens and the city which you described
yesterday as in myth, and we will posit that your city is Athens

and we will say that your citizens are those real ancestors of ours whom the priest described. They will fit exactly, and there will be no disharmony if we say that they were the men who lived at that time. We will divide the work between us and try to fulfil your instructions to the best of our ability. So tell us, Socrates, do you think this story will suit our purpose, or must  e we look for another instead?

SOCRATES: What better choice could there be, Critias? Your story is particularly well suited to the present festival of the Goddess, with whom it is connected, and it is hugely important, I suppose, that it is not a fabricated myth but a true account. How and from where shall we find an alternative if we abandon it? No, you must tell it and good luck to you; and I can take it easy and listen to you reciprocate the accounts I gave yesterday.  27a

CRITIAS: Here then, Socrates, is the plan we have made to entertain you. We thought that Timaeus, who knows more about astronomy than the rest of us and who has devoted himself particularly to studying the nature of the universe, should speak first, and starting with the coming into being of the cosmos bring the story down to the nature of man. I will follow him, assuming that human beings have come into existence as he has described and that some of them have had your excellent education; these I will bring before us as jurors in  b accordance with Solon's account and law,[7] claiming for them citizenship of this city on the basis of their being the Athenians of those days whose disappearance is accounted for in the priestly writings. I shall in the rest of what I have to say assume that I am speaking of citizens who were also Athenians.

SOCRATES: I look like getting a splendid feast of words in return for mine. It falls to you then, Timaeus, it seems, to speak next, after the customary invocation to the gods.

### 3. Prelude. *The distinction between being and becoming; the world has come into being as a likeness of eternal being; our account of it can therefore be no more than 'likely'.*

c    TIMAEUS: Yes, Socrates; of course everyone with the least sense always calls on god at the beginning of any undertaking, small or great. So surely, if we are not quite crazy, as we embark on our account of how the universe came into being, or perhaps had no coming into being, we must pray to all the gods and goddesses that what we say will be first of all according to their

d    mind, and consequently to our own. Let that be our invocation to the gods: but we must invoke our own powers too, that you may most easily understand and I most clearly expound my thoughts on the subject before us.

We must in my opinion begin by making the following distinctions. What is that which always is, and has no becom-

28a   ing, and what is that which is always becoming but never in any way is? The one is apprehensible by intelligence with an account, being always the same, the other is the object of opinion together with irrational sense perception, becoming and ceasing to be, but never really being. In addition, everything that becomes must do so owing to some cause; for nothing can come to be without a cause. Whenever, then, the craftsman of anything keeps his eye on the eternally unchanging and uses

b    some such thing as his pattern for the form and function of his product the result must be good; whenever he looks to something that has come to be and uses a model that has been generated, the result is not good.

As for the whole heaven – let us call it that or 'the world' or any other name most acceptable to it – we must ask about it the question one has to ask to begin with about anything: whether it always was and had no origin of coming into being, or whether it has come into being, having started from some origin. The answer is that it has come into being; for it is visible, tangible and corporeal, and all such things are perceptible by the senses, and, as we saw, perceptible things are objects of

c    opinion and sense perception and come into being and are generated. And it is necessary, we said, for what has come into being to have done so by some cause. To discover the maker and father of this universe is indeed a hard task, and having found him it would be impossible to tell everyone about him. Let us return, then, and ask the following question about it: to     29a which pattern did its constructor work, that which remains the same and unchanging or that which has come to be? If this world here is beautiful and its maker good, clearly he had his eye on the eternal; if the alternative (which it is blasphemy even to mention) is true, then on something that has come into being. Clearly he had his eye on the eternal: for the world is the fairest of all things that have come into being and he is the best of causes. In this way it must have been crafted on the pattern of what is apprehensible by reason and understanding and eternally unchanging. These things being so, it is in every way     b necessary that this world is a likeness of something. Now it is always most important to begin according to the natural beginning. So, on the subject of a likeness and its model, we need to make the following distinction. The accounts are of the same kind as the very things of which they are interpreters. So the accounts of that which is stable and certain and transparent to intelligence are stable and unchanging – they should be irrefutable and invincible to the extent that it belongs to accounts to be so – while the accounts of what has been made     c as a likeness of that thing, in so far as they are of a likeness, are themselves likely and stand in an analogy to those other accounts, namely, whatever being is in relation to becoming, this truth is in relation to conviction. Don't therefore be surprised, Socrates, if often concerning many matters – the gods and the coming into being of the universe – we show ourselves unable to render accounts that are, in every respect and completely, consistent with themselves and accurate. Rather, you must be satisfied if our accounts are no less likely than anybody else's, remembering that both I, the speaker, and you, the     d judges, have a human nature. So it is right that in these matters you should accept the likely myth and look no further than this.

SOCRATES: Excellent, Timaeus; we must accept it exactly as

you say. You have given us a wonderfully acceptable prelude; now go on to develop your main theme.

## MAIN SECTION I.

## THE WORK OF REASON.

*4. The reason for the creation; the world as a living being, modelled on a unique, perfect and eternal living being.*

TIMAEUS: Now, let us state the reason why becoming and
e  this universe were framed by him who framed them. He was good, and what is good never has any particle of envy in it whatsoever; and being without envy he wished all things to be as like himself as possible. This indeed is the most proper
30a  principle of becoming and the cosmos and as it comes from wise men one would be absolutely right to accept it. God therefore, wishing that all things should be good, and so far as possible nothing be imperfect, and finding the visible universe in a state not of rest but of inharmonious and disorderly motion, brought it to order from disorder, as he judged that order was in every way better. It is unlawful for the best to produce anything but the most beautiful. As a result of reasoning, he
b  found that among all things that are by nature visible, no work without intelligence will ever be more beautiful than one with intelligence, if we compare them whole for whole, and that it is impossible for something to gain intelligence without a soul. Because of this reasoning he fashioned the universe by implanting intelligence in soul and soul in body, and so ensured that his work should be by nature the fairest and the best possible. And so the likely account must say that this world
c  came to be in very truth, through god's forethought, a living being[8] with soul and intelligence.

On this basis we must proceed to the next question: What was the living being in the likeness of which the creator constructed the world? We cannot suppose that it was any creature that is by its character naturally such as to be part of a whole, for nothing can be good that is modelled on something incomplete. So let us assume that it resembles as nearly as possible that of which all other beings both as individuals and as kinds are parts, and which comprises in itself all intelligible living beings, just as this world contains ourselves and all visible d creatures. For god, wanting to make the world as similar as possible to the most beautiful and most complete of intelligible things, composed it as a single visible living being, which contains within itself all living beings of the same natural order. 31a Are we then right to speak of one universe, or would it be more correct to speak of a plurality or infinity? ONE is right, if it is to have been crafted according to the model, since that which comprises all intelligible living beings cannot have a double. For there would have to be another living being comprising them both, of which both were parts, and it would be correct to call our world a likeness not of them but of the being which comprised them. In order therefore that our universe should b resemble the complete living creature in being unique, the maker did not create two worlds or an infinite number, but this has become and is and will be the one and only universe.

5. *The body of the world. This is composed of four bodies, earth, air, fire and water, the whole available amount of which is used up in its composition. Its shape is spherical and it revolves on its axis.*

Now anything that has come to be must be corporeal, visible and tangible: but nothing can be visible without fire, nor tangible without solidity, and nothing can be solid without earth. So god, when he began to put together the body of the universe, made it of fire and earth. But it is not possible to combine two things properly without a third; for there has to be some bond c in the middle to hold them together. And the finest bond is one that effects the closest unity between itself and the terms it is combining; and this is best done by a proportion. For whenever you have three numbers or bulks or powers with a middle term 32a such that the first term is to it as it is to the third term, and conversely what the third term is to the middle the middle is to

the first term, then since the middle becomes first and last and similarly the first and last become middle, it will follow necessarily that all can stand in the same relation to each other, and in so doing achieve unity together.[9] If then the body of the universe were required to be a plane surface with no depth, one
b  middle term would have been enough to connect it with the other terms, but in fact it needs to be solid, and solids always need two connecting middle terms. So god placed water and air between fire and earth, and made them so far as possible bear the same proportion to each other, so that fire is to air as air is to water, and as air is to water, this water is to earth; and in this way he bound heaven into a visible and tangible whole. So
c  for these reasons and from these four constituents the body of the world was created to be at unity through proportion; and from these the body acquired friendship, so that having once come together in unity with itself, it is indissoluble by any but him who bound it together.

The construction of the world used up the whole of each of these four bodies. For the creator constructed it of all the fire and water and air and earth available, leaving over no part or
d  power of any of them, reasoning in the following way, firstly, so that the living being should as far as possible be a complete
33a  whole of complete parts, and further, so that it should be one inasmuch as there would be nothing left over out of which another such thing could come into being, and finally that it should be ageless and free from disease. For he knew that heat and cold and other things that have powerful effects surround and attack a composite body from without, so causing untimely dissolution, and make it decay by bringing disease and old age upon it. For this reason and by this reasoning he made this world one complete whole, consisting of parts that are all
b  wholes, and subject neither to age nor to disease. The shape he gave it was suitable and akin to its nature. A suitable shape for a living being that was to contain within itself all living beings would be a figure that contains all possible figures within itself. Therefore he turned it into a rounded spherical shape, with the extremes equidistant in all directions from the centre, the figure that of all is the most complete and like itself, as he judged

likeness to be incalculably superior to its opposite. And he gave
it a perfectly smooth external finish all round, for many reasons.   c
For it had no need of eyes, as there remained nothing visible
outside it, nor of hearing, as there remained nothing audible;
there was no surrounding air which it needed to breathe in, nor
was it in need of any organ by which to take food into itself
and discharge it later after digestion. Nothing was taken from
it or added to it, for there was nothing that could be; for it
supplied its own nourishment from its own decay, and by craft
it had come into being in such a way that it suffered and did    d
everything in itself and by itself, as its constructor thought
that it would be better being self-sufficient than dependent on
anything else. He did not think there was any purpose in attach-
ing hands to it as it had no need to grasp anything or defend
itself, nor with feet or any other means of support. For he
allotted it the motion proper to its body, which of the seven    34a
motions[10] is the one which especially attaches to intelligence
and wisdom, and by leading it around he made it move in a
circle, spinning uniformly around its own axis on the same
spot; any deviation into movement of the other six kinds he
entirely precluded. And because for its revolution it needed no
feet he created it without feet or legs.

Having completed this entire reasoning about the god that
was going to be at some time, the god that always is made    b
it smooth and even all over, with every point on its surface
equidistant from the centre, a body whole and complete, whose
components were also complete bodies. And he put soul in the
centre and stretched it throughout the whole and covered the
body within it. So he established one heaven only, round and
moving around, solitary but because of its excellence needing
no company other than itself, and satisfied to be its own
acquaintance and friend. His creation, then, for all these
reasons, was a blessed god.

*6. The soul of the world. The material of the soul is
mixed and given the appropriate mathematical
structure. It is described as forming a long strip, which
is then cut up into narrower strips, and bent to form
two moving rings, the circles of the same and of the
different. The circle of the same moves the fixed stars,
while the circle of the different, being subdivided into
seven, accounts for the motions of the sun, moon and
five planets. The world-soul is engaged in a perpetual
process of thinking about both the sensible and
intelligible realm, the circles of the same and different
playing a vital part in that process.*

*In writing of the strips that are to carry the planets
Plato probably had in mind, or before him, an
astronomical model of the kind known as an 'armillary
sphere'.*[11]

God did not of course contrive the soul later than the body, as
c  it appears in the narrative we are attempting; for when he put
them together he would never have allowed the older to be
ruled by the younger. There is in us a large element of the
contingent and the random, and we speak correspondingly. But
god created the soul before the body and gave it precedence
both in time and value, and made it the dominating and control-
ling partner. And he composed it in the following way and out
35a  of the following constituents. From the indivisible, eternally
unchanging being and the divisible being that comes to be in
bodies he mixed a third kind of being intermediate between
them; again with the same and the different he made, in the
same way, compounds intermediate between their indivisible
element and their bodily and divisible element; and taking these
three components he mixed them into single unity, forcing the
b  different, which was by nature difficult to mix, into union with
the same, and mixing both with being.[12] Having thus made a
single whole of these three, he went on to make appropriate
subdivisions, each containing a mixture of same and different
and being. He began the whole division as follows. He first
marked off a section of the whole, and then another twice the

size of the first; next a third, half as much again as the second
and three times the first, a fourth twice the size of the second,    c
a fifth three times the third, a sixth eight times the first, a
seventh twenty-seven times the first.[13] Next he filled in the     36a
double and treble intervals by cutting off further sections and
inserting them in the gaps, so that there were two mean terms
in each interval, one exceeding one extreme and being exceeded
by the other by the same fraction of the extremes, the other
exceeding and being exceeded by the same numerical amount.
These links produced intervals of $\frac{3}{2}$ and $\frac{4}{3}$ and $\frac{9}{8}$ within the    b
previous intervals, and he went on to fill all intervals of $\frac{4}{3}$ with
the interval $\frac{9}{8}$; this left, as a remainder in each, an interval whose
terms bore the numerical ratio of 256 to 243. And at that stage
the mixture from which these sections were being cut was all
used up.[14]

He then took the whole composite and cut it down the middle
into two strips, which he placed crosswise at their middle points
to form a shape like the letter X; he then bent the ends round    c
in a circle and fastened them to each other opposite to the point
at which the strips crossed. And having endowed them with
uniform motion in the same place, he made one of the circles
the inner and the other the outer. He declared the outer movement that of the nature of the same, and the inner that of the
nature of the different. The circle of the same he caused to
revolve from left to right, and the circle of the different from
right to left on an axis inclined to it; and he made the master    d
revolution that of the same and similar. For he left the circle of
the same whole and undivided, but slit the inner circle six times
to make seven unequal circles, whose intervals were double or
triple, three of each; and he ordered these circles to revolve in
contrary senses relative to each other, three of them at a similar
speed, and four at speeds different from each other and from
that of the first three but related proportionately.[15]

And when the whole composition of the soul had been
finished to the mind of its composer, he proceeded to fashion
the whole corporeal world within it, fitting the two together    e
centre to centre; and the soul was woven right through from
the centre to the outermost heaven, which it enveloped from

the outside and, revolving on itself, provided a divine principle
of unending and rational life for all time. The body of the
heaven has come into being visible, but the soul is invisible and
37a participating in reasoning and harmony, having, by the best of
the intelligible and eternal beings, come into being as the best
of all generated things. And because it is compounded of the
nature of the same, and the nature of the different, and being
as its three constituent parts, and because it is divided up and
bound together in proportion, and is revolving upon itself,
whenever the soul comes in contact with something whose
being is either dispersed or indivisible, it is moved throughout
b itself and pronounces whatever something is the same as and
whatever it is different from, that is, exactly in what respect
and in what way and how and when each thing happens to be
and undergo change in relation to each other thing, both as
regards the things that come into being and as regards those
that are always the same. And whenever an account which
becomes true in the same way, whether it be about the different
or about the same, and is carried along in the self-moved without speech or sound, whenever such an account becomes
centred on the sensible, and the circle of the different, running
right, reports it to the whole soul, then there arise opinions and
c convictions that are certain and true; but if it is about the
rational, and the circle of the same, running smoothly, declares
it, then the result must necessarily be intelligence and knowledge. And if anyone calls that in which this pair takes place
anything but soul, he is speaking anything but the truth.


7. *Time. The world cannot be eternal, like its pattern;
instead, it exists in time, which is a 'moving image of
eternity' and which is measured and defined by the
movement of the sun, moon and planets. These are now
created and set in the various orbits, or circles of the
different, described in the previous section.*

When the father who had begotten it perceived that the universe
was alive and in motion, an image of the eternal gods,[16] he was
d glad, and in his delight planned to make it still more like its

pattern; and as this pattern is an eternal living being, he set out to make the universe resemble it in this way, as far as was possible. The nature of the living being was eternal, and it was not possible to bestow this attribute fully on what is created; but he determined to make a moving image of eternity, and so, when he orders the heavens, he makes in that which we call 'time' an eternal image, progressing according to number, of an eternity that rests in unity.[17] For before the heavens came e into being there were no days or nights or months or years, but he devises their coming into being at the same time as the heavens are put together;[18] for they are all parts of time, just as 'was' and 'will be' are also forms of it, which we wrongly attribute, without thinking, to the eternal being. For we say of it that it *was* and *will be*, but on a true reckoning we should 38a only say *is*, reserving *was* and *will be* for the coming into being that progresses in time: for both are motions, but that which is eternally the same and unmoved can be neither becoming older nor younger owing to the lapse of time; nor did it ever become so, nor has it now become so, nor can it come to be so in the future; nor in general can any of the attributes which becoming attached to the things that are conveyed in sense perception belong to it, for these have come into being as forms of time which in its measurable cycles imitates eternity. Besides, we use such expressions as what has become *is* what has become, what b is becoming *is* becoming, what will become *is* what will become, and what is not *is* not, none of which is accurate, though this is perhaps not a suitable occasion to go into the question in detail.

So time has come into being with the heavens in order that, having come into being together, they should also be dissolved together if they are ever dissolved; and time has come into being in accordance with the model of the everlasting nature, so that it would be as like the model as possible. For the model is a c being for all eternity, while the heaven correspondingly has been and is and will be throughout the whole extent of time. As a result of god's having this sort of plan and purpose for the creation of time, in order that time might be born, the sun and moon and the five 'planets', as they are called, have come into

being to define and preserve the measures of time. And when
he had made a body for each of them, god set the seven of them
d in the seven orbits of the circle of the different. The moon he
set in the orbit nearest the earth, the sun in the next and the
morning star and the one called sacred to Hermes in orbits
which they complete in the same time as the sun does his, but
with a power of motion contrary to his;[19] consequently, the
sun, Hermes and the morning star all alike overtake and are
overtaken by each other. For the rest, if one were to describe
e in detail where god set them and for what reasons, it would
involve more attention to a side issue than is justified; the topic
is one with which we might deal as it deserves at some later
time when we have leisure. Anyhow, when the beings jointly
needed for the production of time had been given their appropriate motion and they had become living creatures with their
bodies bound by the ties of soul and had learnt their ordained
tasks, they started to move with the motion of the different,
39a which traverses that of the same obliquely and is subject to it,[20]
some in larger circles, some in smaller, those with the smaller
circles moving faster, those with the larger moving more slowly.
And so the movement of the same caused the bodies which
move fastest to appear to be overtaken by those that move most
slowly, though they are in fact overtaking them; for because
their movements are a combination of two distinct contrary
motions, it gave them a spiral twist and made the body which
b falls behind it most slowly (its own motion being the most rapid
of all) seem to keep pace with it most closely.[21] And in the
second of the orbits from the earth god lit a light, which we
now call 'the sun', to provide a clear measure of the relative
speeds of the eight revolutions,[22] to shine throughout the whole
heaven, and to enable the appropriate living creatures to gain
a knowledge of number from the uniform movements of the
c same. In this way and for this reason there came into being
night and day, the period of the single and most intelligent
revolution; the month, complete when the moon has been round
her orbit and caught up with the sun again; the year, complete
when the sun has been round his orbit. Only a very few men
have thought about the periods of the other planets; they have

no name for them and do not calculate their numerical relation-   d
ships. They are indeed virtually ignorant of the fact that their
wandering movements are time, so bewildering are they in
number and so amazing in intricacy. None the less it is possible
to perceive that the perfect temporal number completes the
perfect year when the relative speeds of all eight orbits have
been achieved together and have then reached their completion,
measured by the regularly moving orbit of the same.[23] In this
way and for this purpose the stars which turn back in their
course through the heavens were made, so that this world   e
should in its imitation of the eternal nature resemble as closely
as possible the perfect intelligible living creature.

8. *Living creatures. There are four kinds of living
creature: gods, birds, water animals, land animals. In
this part of his account Timaeus deals only with gods,
and, among land animals, men. The remainder are dealt
with briefly at the end of the dialogue (91d–92c). (a)
There are two kinds of god: (1) the heavenly bodies,
which have already largely been dealt with, and the
earth; (2) the gods of traditional mythology, for whom
we are referred to the traditional sources.*

So far, up to the birth of time, the world had been wrought in
imitation of its model except in one respect: that all living
creatures had as yet not been brought into existence within it.
He therefore went on to make it resemble its model in this
also. He decided that it should have as many forms of life as
intelligence discerns in the perfect living creature. There are
four of these: the heavenly race of gods, the race of winged
creatures that travels by air, the sort that lives in water, and the   40a
sort that has feet and lives on dry land. The divine form he
made mostly of fire so that it should be as bright and beautiful
to look at as possible; and he made it spherical like the universe
and set it to follow the movement of the highest intelligence,
distributing it round the circle of the heaven, to be a true
adornment[24] for it embroidered over the whole. And he gave
each divine being two motions, one uniform in the same place,

b  as each is itself always thinking the same thoughts about the same things, the other forward, as each is subject to the movement of the same and uniform; but he kept them unaffected by the other five kinds of motion, that each might be as perfect as possible. For this reason have come into being the fixed stars, which are living beings, divine and eternal, and remain always rotating in the same place and the same sense; the planets that turn and are characterized by this kind of wandering have come into being in the way previously described. And the earth, our

c  foster-mother, winding[25] as she does about the axis of the universe, he devised to be the guardian and maker of night and day, and first and oldest of the gods born within the heaven. It would be useless without a visible model to talk about the figures of the dance of these gods, their juxtapositions and the relative counter-revolutions and advances of their orbits, or to describe their conjunctions or oppositions, and how they periodically hide each other from us, disappear and then

d  reappear, sending fears and omens of what is to come to those not able to calculate their movement: so let what we have said be enough and let us conclude our account of the nature of the visible created gods at this point.

It is beyond our powers to know or tell about the birth of the other divinities; we must rely on those who have told the story before, who claimed to be children of the gods, and presumably knew about their own ancestors. It is impossible to

e  distrust the children of gods, even if they give no likely or necessary proofs of what they say: we must conform to custom and believe their account of their own family history. Let us therefore follow them in our account of the birth of these gods. Ocean and Tethys were the children of Earth and Heaven, and

41a  their children were Phorcys and Cronos and Rhea and their companions; and from Cronos and Rhea were born Zeus and Hera and their brothers and sisters whose names we know, and they in turn had yet further children.

## 8. (b) The human soul and body. Address to the gods, who are to frame the body and the mortal soul for humans, while their immortal soul is to be created by the demiurge himself.

Anyhow, when all the gods were born, both those whose circuits we see in the sky and those who only appear to us when they wish, the father of this universe addressed them as follows: 'Gods among gods, works whose maker and father I am, what was created by me cannot be dissolved without my consent.[26] Anything bonded together can of course be dissolved, though only an evil will would consent to dissolve anything whose composition and state were good. Therefore, since you have been created, you are not entirely immortal and indissoluble; but you will never be dissolved nor taste death, as you will find my will a stronger and more sovereign bond than those with which you were bound at your birth. Hear therefore what I now make known to you. There are three kinds of mortal creature yet uncreated, and unless they are created the world will be incomplete, as it will not have in it every kind of living creature which it must have if it is to be sufficiently complete. But if these were created and given life by me, they would be equal to gods. In order therefore that there may be mortal creatures and that the whole[27] may be truly a whole, turn your hands, as is natural to you, to the making of living things, taking as your model my power when I created you. And in so far as there ought to be something in them that shares the name with the immortals, something called "divine" and guiding those of them who are always ready to follow you and justice, I will begin by sowing the seed of it and then hand it on to you; it remains for you to weave mortal and immortal together and create living creatures. Bring them to birth, give them food and growth, and when they perish receive them again.'

## 9. The composition and destiny of the human soul.

So speaking, he turned again to the same bowl in which he had mixed the soul of the universe and poured into it what was left

of the former ingredients, mixing them in much the same
fashion as before, only not quite so pure, but in a second and
third degree. And when he had compounded the whole, he
e  divided it up into as many souls as there are stars, and allotted
each soul to a star. And mounting them on their stars, as if on
chariots, he showed them the nature of the universe and told
them the laws of their destiny. To ensure fair treatment for each
at his hands, the first birth would be one and the same for all
42a  and each would be sown in its appropriate instrument of time
and be born as the most god-fearing of living things; and human
nature being twofold, the better kind was that which in future
would be called 'man'. When the souls were of necessity
implanted in bodies, and some part of their bodies was subject
to gain and another to loss, it was necessary that there would
come about, first, perception, the same for all, which arises
from violent affections and is akin to them, and, second, desire
b  mixed with pleasure and pain, and besides these, fear and anger
with the accompanying feelings and their opposites. Mastery
of these would lead to a life of justice, subjection to them to a
life of injustice. And anyone who lived well for his appointed
time would return home to his native star and live his accustomed happy life; but anyone who failed to do so would be
c  changed into a woman at his second birth. And if he still did
not refrain from wrong, he would be changed into some animal
suitable to his particular kind of wrongdoing, and would have
no respite from change and suffering until he allowed the
motion of the same and uniform in himself to draw along with
d  it all that crowd of riotous and irrational feelings that have
grown onto it since its association with fire, water, air and
earth, and with reason thus in control returned once more to
his original and best condition. Having laid down all these
ordinances for them, to avoid being responsible for their subsequent wickednesses, he sowed some of them in the earth,
some in the moon and some in all the other instruments of time;
and what remained to be done after the sowing he left to the
newly made gods, who were to fashion mortal bodies and, for
e  the rest, to devise the necessary additions to the human soul
and their consequences, and so far as they could control and

guide the mortal creature for the best, except, that is, in so far
as it became a cause of evil to itself.

## 10. The confusion caused in the human soul by embodiment, as expressed in terms of the disordering of the circles of the same and different.

Having made all these arrangements, he began resting in his
own accustomed place, as is his wont. While he rested, his
children remembered and obeyed their father's orders, and took
the immortal principle of the mortal creature, and in imitation
of their own maker borrowed from the world portions of fire
and earth, water and air – loans to be eventually repaid – and       43a
welded together what they had borrowed; the bonds they used
were not the indissoluble ones by which they were themselves
held together, but consisted of a multitude of rivets too small
to be seen, which held together in a unity the part of each
individual body. And into this body, subject to the flow of
growth and decay, they fastened the orbits of the immortal
soul. Plunged into this strong stream, the orbits were unable to
control it, nor were they controlled by it, but suffered and
caused violent motions. As a result the whole creature moved,      b
but its progression was disorderly, fortuitous and irrational.
The creatures were subject to all six motions, and so strayed in
all six directions, backwards and forwards, left and right, up
and down. The inward and outward flow of the current which
provided nourishment was strong; but still greater was the
disturbance caused by the affections of the bodies that attacked
them when the body of some creature met with external fire      c
and struck against it or with a solid mass of earth, or liquid
flows of water, or when it was seized by the sudden blast of
driving winds. The motions caused by all these were transmitted
through the body and attacked the soul, and for that reason
were later called, as they still are, 'sensations'.[28] At the time of
which we are speaking the disturbance was at its greatest, and
these motions reinforced the perpetual flow of the body in      d
shaking the orbits of the soul. They completely tied down the
orbit of the same by flowing against it and stopped it from

ruling and going on its way, while violently shaking that of the different. The result was that, though the three pairs of intervals of double and triple, and the connecting middle terms of the ratios three to two, four to three and nine to eight could not be completely dissolved except by him who put them together,

e they were twisted in all directions and caused every possible kind of deflection[29] and damage to the soul's circles, which barely held together, and though they moved, did so quite irrationally, now in reverse, now sideways, now upside down. Something similar happens when a man stands on his head on the ground, pushing his feet against something above him, and what is right and left to him appears reversed to the spectators. This and similar effects were produced in the soul's orbits, and

44a when they encountered anything belonging to the kind of the same or the different in the external world, they made wrong judgements of sameness or difference, and showed themselves wrong and foolish, having at the time no governing orbit in control; for when the external sensations moving and assailing the orbits draw along with them the whole of the soul's container, then the orbits only seem to be in control but are in fact overpowered. And it is indeed because of all these affections

b that today, as in the beginning, a soul becomes irrational when first bound within a mortal body. But when the stream of growth and nourishment flows less strongly, and the soul's orbits take advantage of the calm and as time passes steady down in their proper courses, then the movement of the circles at last regains its correct natural form, and they can name the different and the same correctly and render their possessor sensible. And if at this stage education is added to correct

c nurture, a man becomes altogether complete and healthy and avoids the greatest disease; but if he is careless, after limping through life he returns again to Hades incomplete and unwise.[30] But these things happen at a later time; our present topic still

d needs closer investigation, and we must proceed to give as likely an account as we can of its preliminaries, and set out the divine reasons and forethought by which body and soul were created part by part.

## 11. *The human body: head and limbs.*

The gods copied the round shape of the universe and fastened the two divine orbits of the soul into a spherical body, which we now call 'the head', the divinest part of us which is master of all the rest; they then put together the body and gave the whole thing to the head as its servant, knowing that it would partake of all the varieties of motion there were to be. And to prevent the head from rolling about on the ground, unable to e get over or out of its many heights and hollows, they gave it the body as a vehicle for ease of passage. The body was therefore given height and grew four limbs which could bend and stretch and with which it could take hold of things and support itself, and so by god's contrivance pass through all places, carrying on top of it the seat of our divinest and holiest part. That is the 45a reason why arms and legs grew on us all. And as the gods hold that the front is more honourable and commanding than the back, they made us move, for the most part, forwards. So it was necessary to distinguish the front of man's body and make it different from the back; and to do this they placed the face on this side of the sphere of the head, and fixed its organs for b the soul's forethought in it, and arranged that this, the natural front, should take the lead.

## 12. *The eyes and the mechanism of vision;*[31] *sleep and dreams; mirror-images.*

And the first organs they fashioned were those that give us light,[32] which they fastened there for the following reason. They arranged that all fire which has not the property of burning, but gives out a gentle light, should form the body of each day's light. The pure fire within us that is akin to this they caused to flow through the eyes, making the whole eyeball, and particularly its central part, smooth and close-textured so that it would c keep in anything of coarser nature, and filter through only this pure fire. So when there is daylight round the visual stream, it falls on its like and coalesces with it, forming a single uniform body extending in a straight line from the eyes, along which

the stream from within strikes the external object. Because the
stream and daylight are similar, the whole so formed is affected
d  similarly, and the motions caused by the stream coming into
contact with an object or an object coming into contact with
the stream, the whole transmits right through the body to the
soul and produces the sensation we call 'seeing'. But when the
kindred fire disappears at nightfall, the visual stream is cut off;
for what it encounters is unlike itself and so it is changed and
quenched, being no longer of the same nature as the surrounding air inasmuch as it contains no fire. It ceases therefore to see
e  and induces sleep. For when the eyelids, designed by the gods
to protect the sight, are shut, they confine the power of the fire
within, and this diffuses and smoothes the internal motions,
and produces a calm; when this calm is profound the resultant
sleep has few dreams, but when rather stronger motions remain
46a  images, corresponding in quality and number to the type and
location of the residual motions, are formed internally and
remembered as external events when we wake.[33]

The principles governing reflections in mirrors and other
smooth reflecting surfaces are no longer difficult to understand.
From the communion of the internal and the external fire with
each other, when they have on each occasion become one body
b  on a smooth surface after various transformations, appear of
necessity all such reflections, the fire of the face seen coalescing
with that of the eye on the smooth reflecting surface.[34] And the
right-hand side appears as the left in the image because reverse
parts of the visual stream are in contact with reverse parts of
the object, as compared with what happens in normal vision.
On the other hand, right appears as right and left as left when
c  the light changes sides in the process of coalescing with the light
with which it coalesces, as when the surface of a mirror is
concave and pushes off the right side of the visual stream to the
left and the left to the right. The same mirror turned lengthwise
again, makes the face appear upside down, pushing the bottom
part of the ray upwards and the top part downwards.

## 13. *The distinction between contributory and primary causes, illustrated by the examples of sight and hearing.*

All these are among the contributory causes which god uses as servants in shaping things in the best way possible. But they are thought of by most people not as contributory causes but as   d causes of everything, achieving their effects by heat and cold, solidification and liquefaction, and the like. Yet they are completely incapable of having reason or intelligence; for the only existing thing which properly possesses intelligence we must call soul, and soul is invisible, whereas fire, water, earth and air have all come into being as visible bodies. So the lover of intelligence and knowledge is bound to investigate, first, causes of a rational nature, and, second, those causes that occur when   e things that are moved by some things of necessity move other things. Our procedure must be the same. We must deal with causes of both sorts, distinguishing those that with intelligence are craftsmen of what is beautiful and good from those which when deprived of wisdom on each occasion bring about a random disordered result. As far as the eyes are concerned, we have said enough about the causes which contribute to their having the power they now possess; we must go on to describe the function that makes them most beneficial, because of which god has given them to us. For I reckon that sight has become   47a the cause of the greatest benefit to us in that not a word of all that is being said now about the universe would ever have been said if we had not seen stars and sun and heaven. As it is, the sight of day and night, the months and returning years, the equinoxes and solstices, has caused the invention of number, given us the notion of time and made us inquire into the nature   b of the universe; thence we have derived philosophy, the greatest gift the gods have ever given or will give to mortals. This is what I call the greatest good our eyes give us. There is no need to recite the lesser goods, which 'anyone who is not a philosopher and had lost his sight might lament in vain';[35] let us rather say that this is the cause of this to these ends: god devised sight and gave it to us so that we might see the revolutions of intelligence in the heavens and use their untroubled

course to guide the troubled revolutions in our own understand-
c ing, which are akin to them, and so, by learning what they are
and how to calculate them accurately according to their nature,
correct our own straying revolutions by imitating the altogether
unstraying revolutions of god. The same applies again to sound
and hearing, which were given by the gods for the same end
and purpose. Speech was directed to just this end, to which it
makes an outstanding contribution; and all audible musical
d sound[36] is given us for the sake of harmony, which has motions
akin to the orbits in our soul, and which, as anyone who
makes intelligent use of the arts knows, is not to be used, as is
commonly thought, to give irrational pleasure, but as a heaven-
sent ally in reducing to order and concord any disharmony that
has arisen in the revolutions within us. Rhythm, again, was
e given us from the same heavenly source to help us in the same
way; for most of us lack measure and grace.

## MAIN SECTION II.
## THE WORK OF NECESSITY.

14. *The world is the product not of reason alone, but
of the combination of reason and necessity. We must
therefore make a fresh start and examine the working
of necessity.*

In almost all we have said we have been demonstrating what
was crafted through intelligence; but beside reason we must
48a also set the things that come about through necessity. For this
world came into being from a mixture and combination of
necessity and intelligence. Intelligence ruled over necessity by
persuading it to lead most of the things that come about to
the best result, and it was by this submission of necessity to
reasonable persuasion that this universe here was originally
constituted as it is. So that to give a true account of how it
came to be on these principles one must mix in the kind of the
b wandering cause and how it is its nature to cause motion.

We must therefore retrace our steps, and find another suitable principle for this part of our story, and begin again from the beginning as we did before. We must, that is, consider what was the nature of fire, water, earth and air before the coming into being of the world and what were their attributes before then. For no one has yet indicated their coming into being, but we talk to people as if they knew what fire and each of the others are, and treat them as the letters of the universe, whereas c they ought not properly to be likened even to syllables by anyone with the least sense. Our own position may therefore be described as follows. It is not for us to state the principle or principles of all things or whatever seems to be true of them, if for no other reason than because it is difficult to set forth one's views according to the present manner of exposition. You must not therefore expect such an account from me, nor could I persuade myself that I would be right to undertake a task of such magnitude. I shall stick to the value of the likely accounts d which I laid down at the start, and try to give an account of everything in detail from the beginning that will be no less likely than another man's, but rather more so. So let us begin again, calling also now at the beginning of our speech on a saviour god to see us safely through a strange and unusual argument to e a likely conclusion.

## 15. *The receptacle of becoming.*

Let the new starting point of our account of the universe be a fuller division than the previous; we then distinguished two kinds – we must now point out a third. Two were enough at an earlier stage, when we postulated one kind for the intelligible and unchanging model and another for the imitation of the 49a model which comes into being and is visible. We did not distinguish a third kind, considering two would be enough; but now the argument seems to compel us to try to bring to light in words a kind that is difficult and obscure. What must we suppose its powers and nature to be? Most of all something like this: it is the receptacle and, as it were, the nurse of all becoming. But

true as this is, it needs a great deal of further clarification, and
b   that is difficult, especially because it requires us first to discuss
a problem about fire and the other bodies.

## 16. *The ever-changing appearances of fire, air, water, earth and their lack of substantiality.*

For it is difficult to give a persuasive and certain account of
which of the bodies we really ought to call 'water' rather than
'fire', or indeed which we ought to call by any name rather than
by another or even by all four. How then and in what terms
can we reasonably express our difficulty? Let us begin with
what we now call 'water'. We see it, as we suppose, solidifying
c   into stones and earth, and again dissolving and dispersing into
wind and air; air by combustion we see becoming fire, and fire
in turn when extinguished and condensed taking the form of
air again; air we see contracting and condensing into cloud and
mist, and these when still more closely compacted becoming
running water, which again we see turning into earth and
stones. So they pass coming into being on to each other, it
d   seems, in a cycle. Since therefore none of them ever present
themselves as the same, it would be embarrassing to insist
stubbornly that any of them is certainly this rather than another
thing. On the contrary, we shall be safest by far if we speak
about them on the following assumptions. What we always see
coming into being at different times and in different places, as
we do in the case of fire, we should on each occasion call fire
not 'this' but 'what is such';[37] nor should we call water 'this'
but always 'what is such'; nor should we speak of anything else
e   as having any firmness, all those things which we point to
using the word 'this here' and 'this' thinking that we indicate
something; for it flees, eluding the expression 'this here' or 'this'
or any other that marks the things off as being stable.[38] We
should not say that each of these is 'this', but, rather, 'what is
such', as it is continually recurring as similar, we should refer
to in this way; so we should call fire 'what is continually such'
and everything else in process of becoming.[39] We should only
50a  use the expression 'this thing' or 'that thing' when speaking of

that coming to be in which each of them on each occasion appears and from which it again vanishes; we should never apply the term to any 'some such', to hot or cold, for example, or any other contraries, or to any composites of these.

17. *The receptacle compared to a mass of plastic material upon which differing impressions are stamped. As such it has no definite character of its own.*

But I must try to explain the point again more clearly. Suppose a man is modelling geometrical shapes of every kind in gold, and constantly remoulding each shape into another. If anyone were to point to one of them and ask what it was, it would be     b much the safest, if we wanted to tell the truth, to say that it was gold and never to speak of the triangles and other figures as 'these', with the implication that they are, because they would be changing as we spoke; rather, we should be content if they even admit of the description 'such' with any surety. The same account applies to the natural receptacle of all bodies. It can always be called the same because it never alters its character-  c istics. For it continues to receive all things, and has never in any way whatsoever itself taken on any shape similar to any of the things that enter it; for it is by nature a matrix for everything, which is moved and refigured by the things which enter it, and because of those things it appears different at different times. And the things which pass in and out of it are images of the eternal beings, which are imprinted from them in a wondrous way that is hard to describe – we will follow this up some other time. For the moment we must reflect on three kinds: that which comes to be, that in which it comes to be, and that from which,     d by being made in its likeness, what comes to be is born. Indeed, we should liken the recipient to the mother, that from which to the father, and what they produce between them to their offspring; and we may notice that, if an imprint is to present the full variety of appearances, the material on which it is to be stamped will not have been properly prepared unless it is devoid of all the characters which it is to receive from elsewhere. For if it were like any of the things that enter it, it would produce     e a bad likeness of a contrary or entirely different nature when it were to receive it, as its own features would shine through. So anything that is to receive in itself every kind of character must be devoid of all character. Manufacturers of scent contrive the same initial conditions when they make liquids which are to receive the scent as odourless as possible; and those who set about making impressions in some soft substance make its surface as smooth as possible and allow no impression at all to remain visible in it. In the same way that which all over itself is going to receive properly and repeatedly all the likenesses of the intelligible and eternal things must in its nature itself be devoid of all character.[40] Therefore let us not say that the mother and receptacle of what has come into being as visible or generally as perceptible is either earth or air or fire or water, or yet any of their compounds or components; but we shall not be wrong if we describe it as an invisible and formless kind, receptive of all, possessed in a most puzzling way of intelligibility and extremely hard to grasp. And so far as we can arrive at its nature from what we have said, the most accurate description would be to say that the part of it which has been made fiery appears as fire, the part which has been made wet appears as water, and other parts appear as earth and air in so far as they receive imitations of these.

## 18. *The separate existence of forms and sensory objects as shown by the difference between intellectual knowledge and opinion.*

But we should pursue our inquiry by argument rather when determining the following question about the three kinds: are there such things as 'fire itself by itself', and all the other things of which we are always speaking in this way, as being severally 'themselves in themselves'? Or are the things we see, and the other things that we perceive through our bodies, the only things that have that kind of reality? Is there nothing at all besides them and are we talking nonsense when we say on each occasion that there is an intelligible form of each thing? Is this merely an empty expression? We ought not to dismiss the issue without trial or examination simply by saying that it is so; nor ought we to embark on a long digression in an already long account. The most appropriate procedure would be to make the important distinction in a few words; and this is how I cast my vote. If intelligence and true opinion are different in kind, then these 'things-in-themselves' certainly exist, forms imperceptible to our senses, but apprehended only by intelligence; but if, as some think, there is no difference between true opinion and intelligence, what we perceive through our body must be taken as the most certain reality. Now there is no doubt that the two are different, because they differ in origin and nature. One is produced in us by teaching, the other by persuasion; one is always accompanied by a true account, the other lacks an account; one cannot be moved by persuasion, the other can; and every man,[41] it must be said, partakes of true opinion, whereas gods and only a small number of human beings partake of intelligence.

19. *Summary description of the three factors, form, sensible object and receptacle, which is now called 'space'.*

If this is so, it must be agreed that one kind is the unchanging form, uncreated and indestructible, neither admitting into itself anything from anywhere nor itself entering anything anywhere, imperceptible to sight or the other senses, the object of intelligence; another kind is that which bears the same name as the form and resembles it, but is sensible, generated, is in constant motion, comes into being in, and vanishes from, a particular place, and is apprehended by opinion together with sense perception; and a third kind is that of space which is eternal and indestructible, which provides a seat for everything that comes to be, and which is apprehended without the senses by a sort of spurious reasoning and is hardly an object of belief – we look at it indeed in a kind of dream and say that everything that exists must surely be somewhere and occupy some space, and that what is nowhere in heaven or earth is nothing at all. And because of this dream state we are not awake to the distinctions we have drawn and others akin to them, and fail to state the truth about the true and unsleeping reality. The truth is that not even this very thing upon which a likeness has come into being belongs to it, but this thing always carries with it an appearance of something else. For this reason it is proper for a likeness to come into being in something else, thereby somehow clinging on to being, on pain of being nothing at all. In contrast, the exact and true account comes to the rescue of what has real being, stating that, so long as two things are d different, they will never become at once one and the same and two by either of them coming to be in the other.[42]

## 20. Description of the primitive chaos.

Let the judgement then as measured by my vote be stated in brief as follows. There are and were also before heaven came into being three distinct items: being, space and becoming. As the nurse of becoming was made wet and fiery, and was receiving the shapes of earth and air, and suffering all the affections e that go with them, its visual appearance varied; but as there was no homogeneity or balance in the forces that filled it, no part of it was in equilibrium, but it swayed unevenly in every direction as it was shaken by the forces, and being moved it in turn shook them. And the things that were moved were constantly being separated and carried in different directions, rather like the contents of a winnowing basket or a similar 53a implement for cleaning corn, in which the solid and heavy stuff is sifted out and settles on one side, the light and insubstantial on another: so at that time were the four kinds shaken by the receptacle, which itself being moved acted as a kind of shaking implement. It separated the kinds most unlike each other furthest away from each other and pushed those most like each other towards the same place, with the result that they came to occupy different regions of space even before they were arranged into an ordered universe. Before that time they were b all without proportion or measure; fire, water, earth and air bore some traces of their proper nature, but were entirely in the state to be expected of anything from which god is absent. Such being their nature when god set about ordering the universe, his first step was to shape them completely according to forms and numbers. We must thus assume as a principle in all we say that god brought them to a state of the greatest possible beauty and goodness, in which they were not before. Our immediate task is to attempt an explanation of the particular c structure and origin of each; the account will be unfamiliar, but you will be able to follow it as you are familiar with the methods of learning by which my demonstration must proceed.

21. *The four bodies and the regular solids.*
*Geometrically, solids are bounded by planes, and the*
*most elementary plane figure is the triangle. Two types*
*of triangle are chosen as the basic constituents of all*
*solid bodies, and four basic solids are constructed from*
*them. Transformation of the bodies one into another is*
*accounted for by three of them being built up from the*
*same type of basic triangle: the fourth (earth) being*
*built up from triangles of the other type cannot be*
*transformed into the remaining three.*

In the first place it is surely clear to everyone that fire, earth, water and air are bodies, and all body has depth. There is every necessity in turn that depth is bounded by surfaces, and all rectilinear surfaces are composed of triangles. All triangles derive from two triangles, each having one right angle and two d acute angles: in one of them these two angles are both half right angles, being subtended by equal sides, in the other they are unequal, being subtended by unequal sides. This we postulate as the principle of fire and the other bodies, proceeding in accordance with the account that combines likelihood and necessity; the principles that are even higher than these are known to god and to men whom god loves. We must proceed to inquire which would be the four most beautiful bodies which, e while unlike one another, are capable of transformation into each other on resolution. If we can find the answer to this question we have the truth about the coming into being of earth and fire and the mean terms between them; for we will never agree with anyone that there are visible bodies more beautiful

than these, each in its type. So we must do our best to construct
four types of body outstanding for their beauty and maintain
54a that we have grasped their nature sufficiently for our purpose.
Of the two basic triangles, then, the isosceles has only one
variety, the scalene an infinite number. We must therefore
choose, if we are to start according to our own principles, the
most beautiful of this infinite number. If anyone can tell us how
to choose a more beautiful triangle for the construction of the
four bodies, we will yield to him as a friend, not an enemy; but
for our part we propose to pass over the rest and postulate one
of the many triangles as the most beautiful, that of which a pair
b compose an equilateral triangle. It would be too long a story to
give the reason, but if anyone tests it and discovers it is not so
we will welcome his victory.[43] So let us assume that these are
the two triangles from which fire and the other bodies have
been constructed, one isosceles and the other having a greater

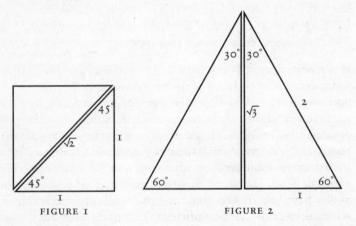

FIGURE 1                              FIGURE 2

The two basic triangles. Cornford suggests that their selection
is determined by 'the choice of the regular solids' for the four
elements; but there is an interesting alternative suggestion in
S. Toulmin and J. Goodfield, *The Architecture of Matter* (Penguin Books, 1965), p. 80.

side whose square is three times that of the lesser. We must now proceed to clarify something we said unclearly a moment ago. It appeared as if all four types of body could pass into each other in the process of becoming; but this appearance is misleading. For, of the four bodies that are produced by our chosen types of triangle, three are composed of the scalene, but the fourth alone from the isosceles. Hence all four cannot pass into each other on resolution, with a large number of smaller constituents forming a lesser number of bigger bodies and vice versa; this can only happen with three of them. For these are all composed of one triangle, and when larger bodies are broken up a number of small bodies are formed of the same constituents, taking on their appropriate figures; and when small bodies are broken up into their component triangles a single new larger figure may be formed as they are unified into a single solid.

So much for their transformation into each other. We must next describe what geometrical figure each body has and what is the number of its components. We will begin with the construction of the simplest and smallest figure. Its basic unit is the triangle whose hypotenuse is twice the length of its shorter side. If two of these are put together with the hypotenuse as diameter of the resulting figure, and if the process is repeated three times and the diameters and shorter sides of the three figures are made to rest in the same point as a centre, the result is a single equilateral triangle composed of six basic triangles. And if four equilateral triangles are put together, three of their plane angles meet to form a single solid angle, the one which comes next after the most obtuse of plane angles;[44] and when four such angles have been formed the result is the simplest solid figure, which divides the surface of the sphere circumscribing it into equal and similar parts.

The second figure is composed of the same basic triangles put together to form eight equilateral triangles, which yield a single solid angle from four plane angles. The formation of six such solid angles completes the second figure.

The third figure is put together from one hundred and twenty

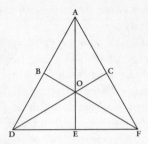

FIGURE 3 'Two of these', e.g. ABO, ACO. 'The resulting figure', e.g. ABOC. The three figures ABOC, DBOE, FEOC coincide at the same vertex O and produce the equilateral triangle ADF.

b basic triangles, and has twelve solid angles, each bounded by five equilateral plane triangles, and twenty faces, each of which is an equilateral triangle.

After the production of these three figures the first of our basic units is dispensed with, and the isosceles triangle is used to produce the fourth body. Four such triangles are put together c with their right angles meeting at a common centre to form a square. Six squares fitted together complete eight solid angles, each composed by three plane right angles. The figure of the resulting body is the cube, having six plane square faces.

There still remained a fifth construction, which the god used for embroidering the constellations on the whole heaven.

With all this in mind, one might properly ask whether the number of worlds is finite or indefinite. The answer is that to d call it indefinite is to express an indefinite opinion where one needs definite information, but that to pause at this point and ask whether one ought to say there is in the nature of things one world or five is reasonable enough. Our own view is that the most likely account reveals that there is naturally a single, divine world; another man considering other factors will come to a different opinion, but he may be dismissed.

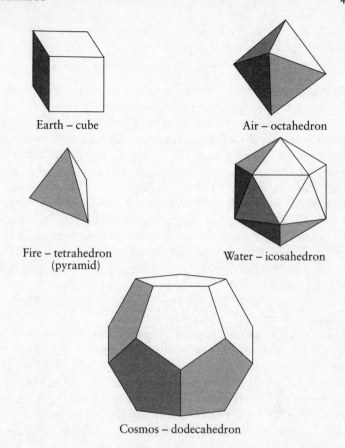

Earth – cube

Air – octahedron

Fire – tetrahedron
(pyramid)

Water – icosahedron

Cosmos – dodecahedron

FIGURE 4 The four figures are the tetrahedron (pyramid), the octahedron, the icosahedron and the cube; the fifth the dodecahedron. The dodecahedron cannot be constructed out of the basic triangles, and because it approaches the sphere most nearly in volume is associated here with 'the whole (spherical) heaven', just as it is associated in the *Phaedo* 110b with the spherical earth. Just how Plato supposed god used it for 'embroidering the constellations on the heavens' we are not told. The Greek word (*diazôgraphô*) means embroidering or drawing figures of living creatures and of course many constellations are named after divine, human or animal figures.

## 22. *Assignment of the four regular solids to the four bodies. Each body is composed of parts of the figure assigned to it, the parts being individually invisible.*

We must proceed to distribute the figures which have just come into being in our account between fire, earth, water and air. Let

e   us assign the cube to earth; for it is the most immobile of the four kinds and the most malleable of bodies, and these are characteristics that of necessity belong to the figure with the most stable faces. And of the triangles we have posited as our principles, the isosceles has a naturally more stable base than the scalene, and of the equilateral figures composed of them the square is, in whole and in part, of necessity a firmer base than

56a  the equilateral triangle. So we preserve the likely account by assigning it to earth, while similarly we assign the least mobile of the other figures to water, the most mobile to fire, and the intermediate to air. And again we assign the smallest figure to fire, the largest to water, the intermediate to air; the sharpest to fire, the next sharpest to air, and the least sharp to water. So to sum up, it is necessary given its nature that the figure which

b   has the fewest faces is the most mobile, as well as the sharpest and most penetrating, and finally, being composed of the smallest number of identical parts, the lightest. Our second figure will be second in all these respects, our third will be third. In accordance with the right account and the likely, let then the solid figure we constructed as a pyramid be the element or seed of fire; and let us say that the second of the figures we constructed is the basic unit of air, the third of water. We must, of

c   course, think of the individual instances of all four bodies as being far too small to be visible, and only becoming visible when massed together in large numbers; and we must assume that when the bodies had been completed with total precision, god fitted together their numbers, movements and other capacities in due proportion, in whatever way the nature of necessity had been persuaded willingly to yield.

## 23. The process of transformation further explained. The main bulk of each body tends to collect in a particular region.

From all we have so far said about the four kinds their behaviour is most likely to be as follows.[45] When earth meets fire it will be dissolved by its sharpness, and, whether dissolution takes place in fire itself or in a mass of air or water, will drift about until its parts meet somewhere, fit together and become earth again; for they can never be transformed into another figure. But when water is broken up by fire or again by air, its parts can combine to make one of fire and two of air; and the fragments of a single particle of air can make two of fire.[46] Again, when a little fire is enveloped in a large mass of air or water or earth and continues its motion in the moving mass, its resistance is overcome and it is broken up, then two particles of fire combine to make a single figure of air; and when air is forcibly broken up two and a half of its figures will unite to make up a single figure of water. In fact we may restate the matter as follows. When one of the other bodies is surrounded by fire and cut up by the sharpness of its angles and edges, the process is halted if it is reconstituted into fire as none of them can effect any change in or suffer any change from what is similar to and identical in character with itself; but the process of dissolution continues so long as in the process of transformation a weaker mass offers opposition to a stronger one. On the other hand, a few smaller particles when surrounded by a mass of larger ones are broken up and extinguished, and the process of extinction ceases if they are prepared to merge into the figure of the predominant mass, when fire turns into air, air into water; but if while they are so merging one of the other basic constituents comes in conflict with them,[47] dissolution goes on until they are either dispersed to their like after complete dissolution under pressure or else mastered and forced to unite with the predominant mass, take on its character and reside with it. It should be added that while undergoing these changes they all exchange places; for owing to the motion of the receptacle the main bulk of each constituent

d

e

57a

b

c

collects in its own separate place, while any part of it which loses its own form and takes on another's is drawn by the shaking to the place of the one whose form it has taken.

## 24. The basic triangles are of more than one size, which accounts for the variety of forms taken by the four bodies.

These are the causes of the coming into being of the pure primary bodies. The presence in each kind of further varieties is due to the construction of the basic triangles. This originally produced triangles not in one size only, but some smaller and some larger, the number of sizes corresponding to the number of kinds within each form. So their combinations with themselves and with each other give rise to endless varieties, which anyone who is to give a likely account of nature must survey.

## 25. Motion and rest are due to dissimilarity and similarity between the four bodies. The circular motion of the world-soul ensures that the bodies keep moving and transforming themselves into each other.

We must also reach agreement about the manner and conditions in which motion and rest arise if the course of our subsequent reasoning is to be clear. We have already said something about them, but must now add that motion can never take place in conditions of uniformity. For it is difficult, or rather impossible, for what is moved to exist without what causes its motion, or what is to cause motion without that which is to be moved; without them there can be no motion and they cannot be in equilibrium. So we must assume that rest and equilibrium are always associated, motion and equilibrium always dissociated; and the cause of disequilibrium is inequality, whose origin we have already described. What we have not explained is how bodies have not been entirely separated off from each other according to kinds and so brought mutual change and motion to an end. The explanation is as follows. The circuit of the whole, within which the constituents are comprised, being spherical and therefore naturally inclined to return on itself, constricts them and allows no space to remain empty. So fire b has achieved the maximum interpenetration of the rest; air the second, having naturally the second finest parts, and so on with the others. For those with the largest parts leave the largest gaps in their texture, and those with the smallest the smallest. So the contraction involved in the process of compression forces the small parts into the gaps left between the large ones. You thus have a process in which small parts are juxtaposed with large ones, and the smaller disintegrate the larger while the larger cause the smaller to combine, and all are carried, up or c down, to their own region; for a change in size involves a change in the position of their region. In this way and for these reasons the disequilibrium always keeps coming into being which ensures that the perpetual motion of the bodies shall continue unceasingly.

## 26. Varieties and compounds of the four primary bodies. Plato has already (57c–d) made provision for their varieties, and he now proceeds to describe some of them, together with some compounds of more than one primary body. (a) Varieties of fire and air.

Next we must notice that several kinds of fire have come into being: flame, the radiation from flame which does not burn but provides the eyes with light, and the glow left in embers after d flame has been quenched. So again with air: there is the brightest variety which we call 'aether', the muddiest which we call 'mist' and 'darkness', and other kinds for which we have no name, but which have come into being because of the unequal sizes of the triangles.

## 26. (b) Water, liquid and 'fusible' (e.g. metals).

There are two main types of water: the liquid and the fusible. The liquid is composed of small and unequal basic units, and so is inherently mobile and easily set in motion by something else because of its lack of uniformity and the shape of its figure. e

The fusible type is composed of large and uniform basic units and is therefore more stable and heavy, its uniformity having compacted it. But fire penetrates and dissolves it and makes it lose its uniformity, and in consequence it becomes more mobile; in that state the pressure of the neighbouring air makes it spread over the ground. The bringing down of the masses is called 'melting' and the spreading over the ground 'flowing'. In the reverse process the fire escapes, but, as it does not pass into a vacuum, it compresses the neighbouring air which in turn compresses the liquid mass, still in a mobile state, into the space left by the fire and mixes the liquid with itself. Under pressure the mass regains its uniformity, seeing that the fire which works non-uniformity is leaving, and settles into its original state. And the loss of fire is called 'cooling' and the contraction which follows is called a state of 'solidity'.

Of all these fusible varieties of water, as we have called them, gold is unique in quality and most highly valued. It is very dense, being compounded of very fine and uniform particles, in colour it is yellow and gleaming, and it solidifies after being filtered through rock. The offshoot of gold, which is very hard because of its density and dark in colour, is called 'adamant'.

Another kind has parts like gold, but has several varieties; it is denser than gold and has a small admixture of fine earth which makes it hard; on the other hand, it is light because it has large interstices in it. This formation is copper, one of the bright and solidified varieties of water. The admixture of earth, when the two separate in course of time, appears on the surface of the metal and is called 'verdigris'.

It would be a simple task to account for the other similar substances, following the principle of the likely myths. And if, for relaxation, a man sets aside the accounts of the eternal beings, and gains pleasure without regret by considering the likely accounts of coming into being, then he adds to his life a measured and sensible pastime. So let us now indulge ourselves and proceed with an account of the likelihoods next in order.

## 26. (c) Mixtures of water. Refrigeration and 'juices'.

We begin with water that is mixed with fire, which is fine and liquid (it owes its name 'liquid' to its motion and the way it rolls over the ground),[48] and also yielding because its bases are less stable than those of earth and give way. This, when left free of fire and air and isolated, becomes more uniform and is compressed by the particles leaving it and is solidified. When   e the process is complete, if it takes place above the earth the result is hail, if on the earth ice; when it is incomplete and the water only half-solidified, the result above the earth is snow, while on earth the consequent freezing of the dew is called 'hoar-frost'.

  Most of the varieties of water are mixtures, which we call generally 'juices', because they are filtered through plants; and   60a because they are mixtures the number of different combinations is large and most of them have no specific name. But there are four named varieties which contain fire and are especially conspicuous: wine, which warms body and soul together; an oily variety, which is smooth and splits the visual ray and is consequently bright and gleaming to the eye and shiny in appearance:[49] pitch, castor oil, olive oil, and other substances with the same power; all varieties which are capable of naturally   b relaxing the pores of the mouth and by this power produce sweetness, to which the general name 'honey' is given; and, lastly, what we call 'acid', which burns and dissolves the flesh, a frothy substance quite distinct from all other juices.

## 26. (d) Varieties and mixtures of earth.

Of the varieties of earth, that which has been strained through water becomes stony substance in the following way. The water mixed with it is broken down in the process of mixture, becomes   c air and thrusts up towards its own region. But the space above it is not empty, and accordingly it thrusts against the neighbouring air. Under the thrust the weight of this air bears upon the mass of earth, compresses it violently and drives it into the place left by the newly formed air. The earth so compressed by

air becomes stone insoluble in water, the finer variety being
transparent and composed of equal and uniform particles, the
poorer varieties being the opposite.

d    When earth loses all its moisture quickly over a fast fire the
product is more brittle, being what we have generically named
'earthenware'. But sometimes there is some moisture left and
the product, black coloured stone, is fusible by fire when it
cools.[50]

There are two other substances formed in the same way when
water has been extracted in large quantity from a mixture; both
are formed of finer parts of earth, both taste salty and both
become only semi-solid and are soluble in water. The one,
e    which cleanses from grease or dirt, is soda; the other, which
blends well in various flavours, is salt, a substance traditionally
beloved of the gods.[51]

Some compounds of earth and water are soluble by fire but
not by water, the reason being as follows. Fire and air do not
dissolve masses of earth, because their parts are smaller than
the interstices in the earth's texture, and so they have plenty
of room to pass through without exerting force and leave it
unbroken and undissolved; but parts of water, being naturally
61a    larger than the interstices, have to force their way through and
so break down the earth and dissolve it. If earth has not been
forcibly compressed, only water will dissolve it in this way; if
it has been so compressed, only fire will dissolve it, for nothing
else can penetrate it. Water again, when under extreme compression, can be dispersed only by fire, but when under less
compression, by both fire and air, air penetrating its interstices,
fire also breaking it down into its triangles. Air under forcible
compression can be resolved only into its elements, when not
so compressed can be dissolved only by fire. Compounds of
b    earth and water behave accordingly. So long as the interstices
in the earth, reduced in size by compression though they be,
are filled with water, parts of water from outside cannot penetrate them and so flow over them and leave them undissolved;
but the parts of fire penetrate the interstices of the water and
have the same effect on it as water has on earth, and are thus
the sole agent that can cause these compounds to dissolve and

melt. Some of them contain less water than earth, namely glass
and all such stones as are called 'fusible'; some have more water,   c
namely substances with a consistency like wax and incense.

## 27. Perceptual affections. (a) Tactile qualities: hot, cold; hard, soft; heavy, light; smooth, rough.

The demonstration of the kinds of substance due to the shapes,
combinations and mutual transformations of the primary
bodies has now more or less been completed. We must go on
to explain how they come to have their affections. Our argument must always presuppose the existence of sense perception,
though we have not yet described the formation of the flesh
and its properties or of the mortal part of the soul. Yet it is   d
impossible to give an adequate account of them without reference to perceptual affections and vice versa; and equally impossible to treat both together. We must therefore assume the
existence of one or other and return later to examine what we
have assumed. To enable us to proceed straight from the kinds
to the affections, let us therefore make the necessary assumptions about body and soul.

Let us first see why it is we call fire 'hot'. We can begin by
calling to mind the dividing and cutting effect of it on our own
bodies; for we all perceive that the affection is a piercing one.[52]   e
The fineness of its edges, the sharpness of its angles, the small-
ness of its particles and its speed of movement – all of which give
it the force and penetration to cut into anything it encounters –
can be explained when we remember the formation of its figure;   62a
and we may conclude that the natural ability to penetrate and
disintegrate our bodies has provided us both with the attribute
and the name of what we now reasonably call 'hot'.[53]

Its opposite is obvious enough, but we must not fail to explain
it. When larger parts of liquids adjacent to the body enter it,
they drive out the smaller parts and, being unable to make their
way into the space thus left, compress the moisture in us, which
instead of being without uniformity and mobile becomes   b
immobile, uniform and compressed, and so solidifies. But what
is subjected to unnatural contraction naturally struggles to

counteract it, and this struggling and shaking is called 'trembling' and 'shivering', and the name 'cold' is given both to the affection as a whole and to what produces it.

'Hard' is anything to which our flesh yields, 'soft' is anything which yields to our flesh; and in this way they are relative terms. c Yielding substances have a small base; but substances which have square bases and so stand firmest retain their shape most stubbornly; so also those most highly compressed are most resistant.

'Heavy' and 'light' can be most easily explained in the context of an examination of the meaning of 'above' and 'below'. For it is quite wrong to suppose that the universe is divided by nature into two opposite regions, one 'below', to which sink all bodies with weight, and one 'above', to which no body rises of d its own accord. For since the universe is spherical, all points at extreme distance from the centre are equidistant from it, and so are by nature all equally 'extremes'; while the centre, being equidistant from the extremes, is equally 'opposite' to them all. This being the nature of the world, it would be inappropriate to use the terms 'above' and 'below' of any of the regions we have mentioned. For it is not right to describe its central region as naturally 'above' or 'below' but simply as the centre; and the circumference is not, of course, at the centre, nor does any part of it differ from any other by being closer to the centre than any part opposite to it. Indeed, can contrary terms be properly applied to any completely uniform object? For if there were a 63a solid in equipoise at the centre, it would never move towards any of its extreme points because of their complete uniformity; while if anyone moved round its circumference he would repeatedly be standing at his own antipodes and so refer to the same point as both above and below. So, since as we have said the whole is spherical, there is no sense in referring to any region of it as 'above' or 'below'. The source of these terms and their proper application, by transference from which we have got into the habit of using them to describe the world as a whole, b we may explain on the following supposition. Imagine a man standing in the region of the universe allotted to fire, to which fire tends to move and in which is the greatest mass of it;

suppose him to be able to detach portions of fire and weigh them in the scales of a balance, which he raises forcibly into the alien air. Clearly it requires less force to raise the smaller c portion than the larger; for when two masses are lifted by the same force the resistance of the larger to the lifting force is by necessity greater than that of the smaller; and the larger will be said to be 'heavy' and to tend 'downwards', the smaller to be 'light' and to tend 'upwards'. This is precisely what we ought to detect ourselves doing in our own region. When we stand on the earth and try to weigh earthy substances, or sometimes pure earth, we lift them into the alien air by force and against their natural tendency, as they cling to the matter kindred to them. So the smaller mass yields more readily than the larger to the d force applied to it and rises into the alien matter; and we call it 'light' and the region into which it is forced 'above', and use 'heavy' and 'below' in the opposite sense. These terms thus necessarily differ relative to each other because the main aggregates of the basic kinds of matter occupy opposite regions to each other; and what is light or heavy or below or above in one e region will be found to be or to become the direct opposite of, or to be at an angle to, or anyway different from, what has these characteristics in another region. The general principle in all these cases is that the journey of any body towards its kindred aggregate makes it 'heavy', and the region to which it moves 'below', while the conditions opposite to these produce opposite results.

So much for our explanation of these attributes. The cause of the attributes smooth and rough I think anyone would be able to understand and explain to someone else. The second is due to a combination of hardness and unevenness, the first to a combination of evenness and density.                                  64a

## 27. (b) Pleasure and pain.

The greatest remaining issue to be dealt with concerning the affections that are common to the whole of the body is the cause of pleasures and pains in the cases we have described, and those affections which, having come to be perceived through the parts of the body, are at the same time accompanied by inherent pains and pleasures.

In any account of the causes of affections perceptible or b imperceptible we must remember the distinction we have already made between substances which are by nature easy or difficult to move; this is the clue which our investigations should follow. For what is naturally mobile, when affected by even a slight impulse, spreads it round, one part passing the same affection on to another until it reaches the consciousness and reports the quality of the agent. By contrast, what is difficult to move is too stable to spread or communicate to its neighbours c the effect of any affection it suffers, and so, as the parts do not pass it on to each other, the original affection does not affect the creature as a whole, which remains unconscious of it. This is what happens with bone and hair and the other parts of our body which are composed mostly of earth; the reverse is true of sight and hearing in particular, as they have in them the highest proportion of the qualities of fire and air. Pleasure and pain, then, we must think of as follows. Any sudden and violent d affection of our natural state is painful, and a sudden return to what is natural is pleasurable; small and gentle affections are imperceptible, their opposites perceptible. An affection which takes place with ease is in the highest degree perceptible, but involves neither pain nor pleasure, for example, the affections of the visual ray itself, which we described earlier as a body formed in daylight cognate with ourselves. No pain is caused by cuts and burns and other affections to which this is subject, e and no pleasure by its return to normal; rather, from its affections and its contact with objects on which it impinges we receive our clearest and most important perceptions; for no violence is involved when it is broken or re-formed. But bodies composed of larger parts, which resist action upon them and 65a transmit its motions to the whole body, are subject to pleasures and pains, pains when their balance is upset, pleasure when it is restored. And bodies subject to wastage and depletion which is gradual, but to sudden large-scale replenishment, are unconscious of the depletion but conscious of the replenishment, and the mortal part of their soul experiences no pain but intense

pleasure – pleasant smells are a good example. But when the
balance is upset suddenly and restored gradually and with diffi-    b
culty the results are the opposite; of this burns and cuts are a
good example.

## 27. (c) Tastes.

That pretty well covers affections common to the body as a
whole and the names given to the agents that cause them. We
must now see if we can account for affections that come about
in particular parts of our bodies, both the affections themselves    c
and their causative agents. We must first explain what we left
out in our account of 'juices', that is, the various affections
peculiar to the tongue. Like most others they are due to contraction and relaxation, but depend more than others on roughness
and smoothness. So when parts of earth enter the discriminat-
ory passages which extend from tongue to heart, melt on con-    d
tact with the moist and soft flesh and contract and dry the
vessels, they produce, if comparatively rough, a sour taste, if
less rough, a dry taste. Substances which rinse the vessels and
wash the entire area of the tongue, if their action is excessive
to the point of dissolving part of its substance, like soda, are all    e
called 'bitter'; but if their action is less violent than that of soda
and the rinsing effect is moderate, they taste salty, and are
agreeable to us without any jarring bitter effect. Things which
absorb warmth from the mouth and are softened by it, become
hot and in turn burn what heated them, and rising because of
their lightness to the sense organs in the head cut everything on
which they impinge, and, because they have this power, are    66a
called 'pungent'. Again there are parts of substances broken
down by decomposition which make their way into the narrow
passages; these parts are duly proportioned to the earthy and
airy parts contained there, which they therefore stir into
motion, causing them to surround each other, one kind of part
finding its way into hollows formed by the other and stretch-    b
ing round it. So hollow films of moisture, either pure or with
an admixture of earth, are formed, and produce liquid air-
containers or hollow spheres of water; these if pure and

transparent are called 'bubbles', if mixed with earth and rising in a mass are spoken of as 'boiling' and 'fermentation'. And

c   what is responsible for these affections is called 'acid'. An affection opposite to all those thus described is produced by an opposite cause. When the composition of the substances entering the mouth in liquid form is akin to the condition of the tongue, they smooth and mollify its roughened parts, and contract or relax, as the case may be, any unnatural relaxation or contraction, restoring its natural state; and any such remedy for violent affections is pleasant and agreeable and has been given the name 'sweet'.

## 27. (d) Smells.

d   So much for tastes. As for the faculty located in the nostrils, its affections display no specific kinds. All odours are half-formed things, and none of our regular figures is commensurate with having any particular odour. The passages of smell are too narrow for earth and water, and too wide for fire and air, so none of them is perceptible to smell; smells occur when substances are in process of liquefaction, decomposition, dissolution or evaporation. They arise in the intermediate stage of

e   the transformation of water into air or air into water. All odours are either vapour or mist; mist is what passes from air into water, and vapour what passes from water into air; so all odours are rarer than water but denser than air. This can be seen when one breathes air in forcibly through something that obstructs the passage of the breath; no odour percolates through, but the

67a air comes through devoid of any odour. These, then, are two groups into which the diversities of odour fall. They have no names and do not consist of a plurality of definite types; the only clear distinction we can make is between the pleasant and unpleasant. The unpleasant roughens and does violence to the whole cavity between crown and navel; the pleasant soothes it and restores it agreeably to its natural condition.

## 27. (e) Sounds.

A third sensory part in us which we must examine is hearing, and we must explain the various affections occurring in it. b Sound may be generally defined as a stroke given by air, through the ears, to the brain and blood and passed on to the soul; and the consequent motion which starts from the head and terminates in the region of the liver is hearing. Rapid movement produces high-pitched sound, and the slower the motion the lower the pitch. Regular motion gives a uniform, smooth sound, irregular motion a harsh sound. Large and small motions pro- c duce loud and soft sounds. Concord in sounds we must deal with later.[54]

## 27. (f) Colours.

There remains a fourth sensory kind which includes within it a large number of diversities that need classification, diversities to which we give the general name 'colour', which is a kind of flame that streams off bodies of various kinds and is composed of parts so proportioned to our sight as to yield sense percep- tion. The bare facts about the causes of vision we have already mentioned. So it would be especially proper and reasonable to d expound on the various colours by way of a reasonable account, as follows.

The parts which impinge on the visual ray from other bodies are either larger or smaller than those of the visual ray itself or else the same size. If they are the same size they are impercep- tible or as we say 'transparent'. If they are larger they compress the ray, if they are smaller they dilate it; these affections are the twins of what is hot or cold to the touch and what is astringent e or burning ('pungent' as we call it) to the tongue, being the same affections produced in a different medium, and appearing for the reasons given with a corresponding difference as 'black' and 'white'. We must assign these names accordingly, calling that which dilates the visual ray 'white' and that which com- presses it 'black'. When another kind of fire with a faster motion falls on the visual ray and penetrates it right up to the eyes, it

68a  forces apart and dissolves the passages in the eyes, and causes
the discharge of a mass of fire and water which we call a
'tear'; this incoming fire meets a fire moving towards it, and the
outgoing fire leaps out like lightning while the incoming is
quenched in the moisture. The result is a confusion of all kinds
of colours; this experience we call 'dazzling' and the object
b  which produces it 'bright' and 'gleaming'.

Then there is a variety of fire intermediate between these
which reaches the moisture of the eye and mixes with it, but is
not 'gleaming'; the radiance of this fire shining through the
moisture with which it is mingled produces a blood-like colour
which is called 'red'.

Bright mixed with red and white produces orange. But in
what measure the quantities should be mixed, it would not be
wise to say, even if one knew; nobody would be even moder-
ately able to state either a necessity or the likely account for
these matters.[55]

c  Red mixed with black and white gives purple, or deep blue
when these ingredients are well burnt and more black added.
Tawny-yellow is a mixture of orange and grey, grey being a
mixture of black and white, while pale yellow is a mixture of
orange and white. White combined with bright and immersed
in deep black produces blue-black, which in turn produces
blue-green when mixed with white, while tawny-yellow and
black yield green.

As for the other colours, it should be fairly clear from these
d  cases to what mixtures they would be likened so as preserve
the likely myth. But to try to apply an experimental test would
be to show ignorance of the difference between human nature
and divine; for god has both adequate knowledge and ability
to mix many things into one and, again, to dissolve one into
many, while no human being either is or will ever be adequate
to either of these tasks.

# MAIN SECTION III.
# REASON AND NECESSITY WORKING
# TOGETHER.

*In the preceding section we have been concerned mostly with those properties and processes of bodies that are necessary given their basic geometrical constitution. These processes are now subordinated to the divine providence, which makes the best out of them that it can. In the remainder of our account we shall be largely concerned with human psychology and physiology.*

28. *The subordinate gods take over from the demiurge the divine principle of soul (cf. 41c–d), encase it in the globe of the skull, and form the mortal parts of the soul out of the affections that the soul necessarily experiences because of the body.*

All these things were naturally so constituted of necessity, and the maker of what is fairest and best among things that come into being took them over when he generated the self-sufficient and most complete god, using this type of cause as subordinate but himself contriving the good in things that come into being. We must therefore distinguish two types of cause, the necessary and the divine. The divine we should look for in all things for the sake of the measure of happiness in life that our nature permits, and the necessary for the sake of the divine, reflecting that without the necessary causes, those other ones, with which alone we are seriously concerned, are not to be perceived, apprehended, or in any other way attained.

The two kinds of cause, which like timber[56] for a carpenter are needed by us to construct the rest of our account, have now been prepared.[57] Let us, therefore, briefly return to our starting point and retrace our steps that led us to the point which we have now once more reached, and then attempt to fit an end

and a 'head' to our myth,[58] one that is in harmony with what
we have said up till now.

   As we said at the beginning, these things were in disorder till
god introduced proportionate relations, internal and external,
among them, to the extent and in the ways that they were
capable of having ratios and proportions. For at first they stood
in no such relations, except by chance, nor was there anything
c  that deserved the names – fire, water and the rest – which we
now use. But he reduced all of them to order, and then put
together this universe out of them, a single living creature containing in itself all other living things moral and immortal. He
made the divine with his own hands, but he ordered his own
children to manufacture the generation of mortals. They took
over from him an immortal principle of soul, and, imitating
him, encased it in a mortal physical globe, with the body as a
d  whole for vehicle. And they built on to it another mortal part,
containing terrible and necessary affections: first pleasure, the
chief incitement to wrong, then pain, which frightens us from
good, furthermore daring and fear, two foolish counsellors,
and anger hard to appease and credulous hope. To this mixture they added irrational sense perception and desire which
shrinks from nothing, and so of necessity composed the mortal
element.

**29. The mortal parts of the soul. Plato assumes the
threefold division of the soul into reason (here called the
'divine' element), spirit and appetite (together referred
to as the 'mortal' element) which he had made in the**
Republic. *Spirit is located in the region of the heart,
appetite in the belly. The function of the various organs
is described: heart and lung, liver and spleen, intestines.*

And since the gods shrank from polluting the divine element
with these mortal feelings more than was absolutely necessary,
e  they settled the mortal element in a separate dwelling in the
body, and constructed the neck as a kind of isthmus and boun-
dary between head and breast to keep them apart. The mortal
element they secured in the breast and trunk (as we call it); and

since it naturally has a better and a worse part, they divided
the hollow of the trunk by inserting the midriff as a partition,
rather as a house is divided into men's and women's quarters.    70a

The part of the soul which is the seat of courage, anger and
ambition they located nearer the head between midriff and
neck, so that it would be well-placed to listen to the commands
of reason and combine with it in forcibly restraining the appetites when they refused to obey the word of command from the
citadel. They stationed the heart, which links the veins and is    b
the source of the blood which is carried forcefully around the
body to all its members, in the guardroom with the following
intention. When the force of anger boils up because reason
reports that some wrong is being done involving the members
of the body – whether by external action or internally by the
appetites – exhortations and threats should pass quickly
through the body's narrow ways, and any sentient part of it
listen obediently and submit to the control of the best. And    c
they devised relief for the throbbing of the heart when dangers
are anticipated or anger is aroused, anticipating that because
of fire all this kind of swelling of the enraged parts would occur.
This was the structure of the lung, which they made soft and
bloodless, full of cavities like a sponge, so that it would, by    d
absorbing breath and drink, act as a coolant and provide relief
and ease from the heat. For this reason they cut the channels of
the windpipe to the lung and set it round the heart like a
cushion, so that when the anger was at its height, the heart
would beat against something yielding, be refreshed, and so
because less distressed better able to assist anger in the service
of reason.

The part of the soul that desires food and drink and other
natural needs of the body they located between the midriff and    e
the region of the navel, building in all of this area a kind of
manger for the nourishment of the body; and they secured this
part of the soul there like a wild beast, which must be fed with
the rest of us if mortals were to exist at all. And they put it in
this position in order that it might continue to feed at its stall,
but be as far as possible from the seat of deliberation, and cause
the least possible noise and disturbance, so leaving the highest    71a

part of us to deliberate quietly about what benefits us all collectively and individually. And knowing that it would not understand reason or be capable of paying attention to rational argument even if it became aware of it, but would easily fall under the spell of images and phantoms by day or night, god
b  played upon this weakness and formed the liver, which he put into the creature's stall. He made it smooth and close in texture, sweet and bitter, so that the power of the thoughts being carried from the intelligence, by being reflected in it as in a mirror which receives in itself the impressions and produces visible images, would cause it to be afraid when it uses the liver's native bitterness and plays a stern and threatening role, quickly infusing the whole organ with bitterness and making it appear in bilious colours; at the same time it contracts the liver and makes it all wrinkled and rough, bending and shrivelling the
c  lobe, blocking and closing the vessels leading to it and so causing pain and nausea. He also made the liver in this way so that when some gentle influence from reason paints appearances of the opposite kind, which will neither produce nor have connection with anything of a contrary nature to their own, and brings relief from bitterness, using the organ's innate sweetness to render it straight and smooth and free, it would make
d  the part of the soul that lives in the region of the liver cheerful and gentle, and able to spend the night in measured activity by having divinatory dreams, as reason and understanding are beyond it. For our makers remembered that their father had ordered them to make mortal creatures as good as possible, and so did their best even with this base part of us and gave it
e  the power of prophecy so that it might have some apprehension of truth. And clear enough evidence that god gave this power to human folly is to be found in our incapacity for inspired and true prophecy when in our right minds; we only achieve it when the power of our understanding is inhibited by sleep, or when we are in an abnormal condition owing to disease or divine inspiration. And it is the function of someone in his right mind to construe what is remembered of utterances made in dream
72a  or waking by the prophetic and inspired nature, as well as the appearances which have been seen, and to discern by reasoning

what good or evil they all portend and for whom, whether future, past or present. It is not the business of any man, so long as he is in an abnormal state, to interpret his own visions and utterances; there is truth in the old saying that only a sane man can attend to his own concerns and know himself. Hence the custom of setting up judges to pronounce judgement on b inspired prophecies; they are sometimes called 'diviners' by those who are ignorant that they are not in fact diviners, but expounders of riddling oracles and visions, and so most exactly called 'interpreters of those who divine'.

It is for this reason, then, that the liver has such a nature as well as the natural location that we claim it has, namely, for the sake of divination. So long as any creature is alive, the liver gives comparatively clear indications, but after death it becomes blind and its signs too obscure to convey any clear meaning. The structure and position of the organ immediately on its left c have come into being in order to keep the liver bright and clean, like a duster kept handy to clean a mirror. For the spleen, whose texture is hollow and bloodless and therefore loose, absorbs and clears away any impurities which occur in the region of the liver because of diseases in the body. When filled with these d impurities it becomes swollen and infected, but when the body is purged it subsides and resumes its original state.

That concludes our account of the mortal and divine parts of the soul, where they are housed and with what organs and why. Only divine confirmation would justify us in insisting on its truth; but we may venture to claim now, and still more on further reflection, that it is likely, so let us do so. Our next topic e must be pursued on the same principles; it is the way in which the rest of the body has come to be. Its constitution can be best viewed with the following considerations in mind. Those who framed our species knew how ungovernable our appetite for drink and food would be, and how we would out of sheer greed consume much more than a moderate or necessary amount; in order therefore to prevent our rapid destruction by disease and the prompt demise of the mortal kind before its completion, 73a they made the lower belly, as it is called, into a receptacle to contain superfluous food and drink, and wound the bowels

round in coils to prevent the quick passage of food, which
would otherwise compel the body to want more and make its
appetite insatiable, so rendering the entire species incapable
through gluttony of philosophy and culture, and unwilling to
listen to the most divine element in us.

## 30. *The main structure of the human frame. The marrow (regarded as life-substance and seed).*

b   Bone, flesh and the other tissues were constituted as follows.
Their starting point was the formation of the marrow; for the
bonds of life, by which the soul is tied together with the body,
being the roots of the mortal creature, are made fast in the
marrow which has itself been formed of other materials. From
each particular type of triangle the god set aside those that were
smooth and unwarped and so able to produce most exactly
c   fire, water, air and earth; these he mixed in due proportion to
produce marrow, as a kind of universal seed for mortal creatures of every kind. In it he firmly implanted the different kinds
of soul, dividing the marrow in his initial distribution into as
many different varieties and the particular forms as it was
destined to bear. And he moulded into spherical shape the part
d   of the marrow (the ploughland, as it were) that was to contain
the divine seed and called it the brain, indicating that when
each creature was completed the vessel containing the brain
should be the head.[59] The rest of the marrow that was to contain
the mortal parts of the soul he divided into long, cylindrical
sections, called by the general name 'marrow', to which the
whole soul was bound, as if to anchors. And round brain
and marrow, for which he first constructed a bony protective
covering, he went on to frame our whole body.

## 31. *Bone, sinews and flesh; distribution of flesh on the frame; skin, hair and nails.*

e   He put bone together as follows. He sifted out earth that was
pure and smooth, kneaded it and steeped it in marrow; next he
placed it in fire and then again into water, then back into fire

and then again into water, and by this repetition of the process rendered it insoluble by either. From the resultant substance he formed a bony sphere to contain the brain, leaving only a narrow outlet; and to surround the marrow in neck and back he moulded vertebrae from it and balanced them like pivots through the whole span of the trunk, starting from the head. The seed was thus entirely fenced in and protected by a stone-like container, jointed to provide for movement and flexibility, in whose construction the power of the different kept the parts distinct. But he thought that the constitution of bone was unduly brittle and inflexible, and that when subjected in turn to heat and cold it would mortify and destroy the seed within it, and for this reason he devised the sinews and flesh. By binding all the limbs together with something that contracts and relaxes about the joints he aimed to enable the body to bend and stretch. The flesh was to serve as a protection against heat and a shelter against cold, besides being a kind of padded garment to cushion us softly and gently against falls; it also contained warm moisture and so was able to provide a cooling system of its own in summer by sweating out this moisture over the whole body, and a measured protection against the assaults of the enveloping frost in winter by its internal warmth. With this in mind he who modelled us like wax composed our flesh, soft and full of sap, by making a suitably proportioned compound of water, fire and earth, and adding a ferment of acid and salt to the mixture; the sinews he made from a mixture of bone and unfermented flesh, producing a substance intermediate between the two and adding a yellow colour. The sinews are thus tenser and tougher than flesh, but softer and more elastic than bone. The two of them the god wrapped round bones and marrow, tying the bones together with sinews, and making a shelter for them all with flesh. To the bones which were most endowed with soul he gave the thinnest covering of flesh, and those least endowed the thickest and most plentiful; and he caused little flesh to grow at the joints of the bones, except where reason showed it to be necessary. His purpose was, firstly, to avoid making the body clumsy and immobile because the flesh hindered the movement of the joints, and,

74a

b

c

d

e

secondly, to avoid making it insensitive because of the thickness of many superimposed layers of flesh, thus hampering memory and sharpness of mind. So thigh and calf, the area around the hips, upper and lower arm, and other bones within the body that are unjointed or devoid of intelligence, because they contain little soul in their marrow, are all well covered with flesh; but parts where there is intelligence are, in general, less well covered, though there are exceptions like the tongue where the flesh is itself formed for the purpose of sense perception. For out of necessity the nature with which we are born and which grows with us in no way allows that thickness of bone and abundance of flesh be combined with quickness of perception. For if these two characteristics had consented to coincide they would certainly have done so in the structure of the head, and with a head fortified with flesh and sinew human life would have been twice or many times as long as at present, as well as healthier and more free from pain. As it was, those who crafted our coming into being weighed up whether to produce a longer-lived but inferior type or a shorter-lived but superior, and decided that a shorter and better life was for everyone in all respects preferable to a longer but poorer one. So they covered the head with thin bone, but not with flesh or sinews, because it had no joints; which is why the head attached to man's body combines a large degree of perceptiveness and intelligence with a much smaller degree of structural strength. On the same principles and in the same way the god fastened sinews uniformly in a ring round the neck at the base of the head, and tied the end of the jaw bones to them just under the face; the remainder he distributed among the various limbs to hold the joints together. Those who arranged our bodies gave the mouth with its teeth, tongue and lips its current order, both for the sake of the necessary and for the best; they designed it as an entry for the sake of the necessary, and as an exit for the sake of the best; for the food it takes in is necessary to nourish the body, what goes out of it is good in the sense that the outgoing stream of speech is the servant of intelligence and so the highest and best of all streams. They were also unable to leave the bone of the skull bare because of the extremes of seasonal heat and cold, but could not let it become dull and insensitive under a heavy shelter of flesh. So without drying up entirely, the flesh 76a formed a loosely fitting film which we now call 'skin'; this film closed in on itself and grew round over the head to cover it owing to the action of the moisture in the brain, which made its way up through the sutures, damped the skin and made it close up into a kind of knot on the crown. (The sutures are of very different patterns owing to the varied action of the revolutions and the nourishing material, being greater or fewer in number according to the intensity of the struggle between b the two.)[60] The divine[61] pricked this covering of skin all over by means of fire, and the moisture made its way out through the perforations. Such of it as was pure liquid and heat escaped, but that mixed with the ingredients from which the skin was made was driven outwards and stretched into a long external thread whose fineness was equal to the size of the puncture; but the pressure of the surrounding air slowed up its motion and c made it coil up under the skin and take root there. This is the natural process that caused hair to grow on the skin; it is a fibrous substance of the same nature as skin, but harder and denser because of the felting process caused by refrigeration, a process which operates on each hair as it emerges from the skin. Our maker thus gave us shaggy heads, using the causes we have just described, but with the intention of providing d another form of shelter than flesh to shield the brain; for hair is light, and provides adequate shade in summer and protection in winter without hindering quickness of perception. And where fingers and toes were finally knitted up, a mixture of sinew, skin and bone combined to form, when dried out, a single hard covering. These were the auxiliary causes used to craft it, but its governing purpose looked to future creations. For those who framed us knew that later on women and the other animals e would be produced from men, and that many creatures would need claws and hoofs for different purposes; so they provided the rudiments of them in men at their first creation, and for this reason and with these motives they caused skin, hair and nails to grow at the extremities of the limbs.

## 32. *Plants.*

The parts and limbs of the mortal creature were thus brought
77a  together into a whole which must of necessity live its life
exposed to fire and air, be worn away and wasted by them, and
finally perish. And to support it the gods devised and made to
grow another nature akin to the human, but with different
forms and senses, another kind of living thing, trees, plants
and seeds. These we have today schooled and domesticated to
our purposes by agriculture, but at first there were only the
b  wild varieties, which are the older of the two. Everything
that has life has every right to be called a living thing; and the
group of which we are speaking has the third sort of soul,
which we have located between midriff and navel, and which
is without belief or reason or understanding but a sense of
pleasure and pain together with appetites. It is always entirely
passive; its formation has not given it the natural[62] capacity to
perceive and reflect on its own experiences, by revolving in and
c  about itself, rejecting motion from without and exercising a
motion of its own. So it is a creature with a life of its own,
but it cannot move and is fixed and rooted because it has no
self-motion.

## 33. *Digestion and respiration.*

When the higher powers had thus made plants grow for us
inferior creatures to feed on, they cut in our body a system of
d  conduits, like water channels in a garden, to irrigate it with
incoming moisture. First beneath the covering of skin and flesh
they cut two veins along the back, like two water pipes, corresponding to the two sides of the body, right and left; these
veins ran down beside the spine, to help the flourishing of the
life-giving marrow which lay between them and to facilitate by
their downward flow the even distribution of moisture to the
rest of the body. Next they cut the veins in the head and wove
e  them through one another in opposite directions, left to right
and right to left, to help the skin in binding the head to the
body as there were no sinews holding it round the crown,[63] and

to ensure that sensations from either side should be conveyed to the whole body.

## 33. (a) The fish-trap

They went on to contrive their irrigation system in a way that we shall best understand if we first agree on the following 78a principle. All bodies composed of smaller parts are impervious to larger ones, but those composed of larger ones are not impervious to smaller; fire is composed of the smallest parts, and consequently penetrates water, earth and air and any bodies composed of them, which cannot remain impervious to it. The same principle must be applied to the belly, which retains the b solids and liquids it receives, but cannot retain air and fire whose parts are smaller than those of its own structure. The god availed himself of this in arranging the irrigation of the veins from the belly. He wove a network of air and fire, like a fish-trap, with two funnels at its entrance, one of which was again double; from the funnels a network of reeds (as it were) extended right round to the far end of the structure. The interior c of the network he made of fire, the funnels and the main framework of air. This structure he took and set it round the living creature he had formed. He inserted the two funnels into the mouth, and extended one of them downwards into the lung by way of the windpipes, and the other alongside the windpipes into the belly. The first channel he split again and brought the two subdivisions out together by way of the nostrils, so that when the other channel by way of the mouth was not working, there would be an alternative source of supply. The main part d of the fish-trap he attached round the hollow of our body, and gave the whole an alternating movement, a flow into the funnels (gentle, as they are made of air) being followed by a flow back, while the network correspondingly sinks in or out through the body, which is porous, and the attached rays of the internal fire follow the movement of air in either direction.[64] This move- e ment continues so long as the mortal creature survives, and is the process to which we say the name-giver gave the names 'inhalation' and 'exhalation'. This whole action and reaction

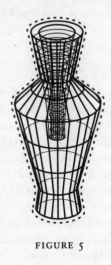

FIGURE 5                                      FIGURE 6

Figure 5: The fish-trap described is constructed on the principle used in the common lobster-pot. But the narrow entrance is contrived by inserting a separate funnel into the main body of the trap. The trap is then transferred to the human body as illustrated in Figure 6. The funnel, internally, leads to lungs and belly, and has a double exit, through mouth and nose, the exit through the nose being again subdivided.

results in our body being fed and kept alive by moisture and refrigeration. For the internal fire follows the movement of the air which it is attached and, as it surges in and out, enters 79a the belly and takes hold of the food and drink there, breaks it up small and disintegrates it, and carries it through the outlets along which it passes, discharging it into the veins like water from a spring into conduits and making the currents in the veins flow through the body as if through an aqueduct.

## 33. (b) Circular thrust.

But let us look again at the process of respiration and see what causes it to take place as it does. Since there is no void into b which a moving body can move, but the breath does move out of our body, it follows clearly that it does not move into a void but displaces the adjacent air. This process of displacement is continuous, and so of necessity the air is thrust round into the space originally vacated by the breath; this it enters and refills, replacing the breath. The process takes place all together at the c same time, like the turning of a wheel, due to there being no void. So the chest and lungs when they expel the breath are filled again by the air surrounding the body, which is driven in through the porous flesh by the circular thrust; and when the flow of air is reversed and moves out through the body it in turn thrusts the breath round and in through mouth and nostrils. The original cause of these processes is as follows. In every creature d the parts close to the blood and the veins are the hottest, constituting a kind of internal source of fire. So in our simile of the fish-trap we said that all the inner parts were woven of fire, the external of air. What is hot, we must agree, naturally moves out to its like in its own region. And as there are two outlets, one through the body, the other through mouth and nostrils, when the hot rushes out in one direction it pushes the air round e in the other direction; and the air so thrust falls into fire and is heated, while the air which moves out is cooled. And as the air which enters by either outlet rises in temperature, it recoils because of its greater heat and moves towards its like, thrusting air round to the other passage. This air again is similarly affected and reacts in the same way, and the two impulses set up a continuous cycle of action and reaction which produces our inhalation and exhalation.

The action of cupping glasses, the process of swallowing and the behaviour of projectiles discharged either into the air or 80a along the ground are to be explained on the same principle; so also are sounds which seem high or low according to their speed of travel and concordant or dissonant according to the similarity or dissimilarity in the motions they set up in us. The

slower sounds when they catch up with the motions of the faster sounds which arrived earlier find these dying away and
b already similar to the motions which they themselves impart on their arrival; when they do arrive their introduction of a fresh motion does not cause discord, but produces an experience in which high and low are blended, because the slow motion now beginning is similar to the faster one just coming to an end. So they give pleasure to fools and true enjoyment to the wise because of the imitation of the divine harmony that has come to be in mortal movements.[65] Other examples are any stream
c of flowing water, the fall of thunderbolts and the puzzling attraction of amber and lodestone. In fact there is no 'attraction'. Proper investigation shows that there is no void and that circular thrust operates in all these instances; the various bodies part or come together in the course of mutual interchanges of position and what seems like magic turns out on proper investigation to be due to the complication of their effects on each other.

d    It is in this way and by these means, as we said before, that the process of respiration takes place, from which this account set out. Fire cuts up our food, and as it ebbs and flows within the body with the motion of the breath, its ebb and flow fill the veins with the cut-up food which it pumps into them from the belly. And by this process it has come to be that the streams of nourishment flow through the whole body in all animals. The
e parts newly cut from kindred substances – fruit and vegetables which god caused to grow to provide food for us – contain all sorts of colours because of the way they were mixed, but are mainly pervaded by a red hue, the natural product of the cutting and staining of the fire in a moist environment. This is how the blood, as we call it, which runs in our body, gets the colour we
81a have described; it feeds the flesh and the whole body, whose parts draw on it to replenish their loss by depletion. Replacement and wastage take place in the same way that the motion of everything in the universe has come to be, namely, that like always moves to like. For the bodies around us are constantly breaking down the human body and distributing each type of constituent to its like; so analogously the constituents of the

blood, broken up small and surrounded by the living organism as by a containing heaven, must of necessity move in imitation b of the universe, each internal fragment moving to its like and replenishing previous wastage.

## 34. Normal growth and decay; natural death.

Decline is caused by excess of wastage over intake, growth by the opposite. And when the structure of the entire creature is young, and the triangles of its constituent elements are new, like a ship straight from the stocks, they are locked firmly c together, though the consistency of the whole aggregate is soft, having been recently formed of marrow and fed on milk. So the triangles composing the food and drink which the structure takes into itself from the outside are older and weaker than those in itself, which are new, and it breaks them up and absorbs them, and so it makes the animal big by nourishing it on many similar triangles. But when the root of the triangles is loosened by fighting numerous combats with many opponents over a long period of time, they can no longer cut up into d their own likeness the triangles of the food taken in, but are themselves easily broken up by the newcomers; and in the process every creature fails and declines into the condition which we call 'old age'. Finally, when the bonds of the triangles in the marrow fail and part under the stress, the bonds of the soul are also loosened; and when this happens in the course of nature the soul departs gladly – for everything that takes place e naturally is pleasant, whereas what is contrary to nature is painful. So a death by disease or injury is painful and forced, but one that brings life to its natural close by old age is of all deaths least distressing and brings pleasure rather than pain.

## 35. Diseases of the body. (a) Diseases due to lack of balance between the four primary bodies.

The origin of diseases should be obvious to everyone. The body is composed of four kinds – earth, fire, air and water; and 82a disorders and diseases are caused by an unnatural excess or deficiency of any of them, by their shifting from their own proper place to another's place, by any part of the body taking in an unsuitable variety either of fire or another kind (for there are several varieties of them), and by similar disturbances. For

b if there is any unnatural formation or change of place, parts that were cold become heated, the dry becomes moist, what was light becomes heavy, and every kind of change takes place. For, as we claim, it is only if the same part is added to the same part or removed from the same part in the same respect and in the same way and proportionately that the body will stay the same and remain safe and sound; any part which when departing or entering strikes a false note in these respects will give rise to all kinds of change, and to endless disease and deteriorations.

## 35. (b) Diseases of the 'secondary formations' – marrow, bone, flesh, sinew, blood.

And as there are secondary formations in nature, there is a

c further study for whoever wants to understand diseases. Marrow and bone and flesh and sinew, and, in a different way, blood, are all composed of those four kinds and though most diseases affecting them are caused in the way just described, the worst disorders are due to deterioration caused by reversal in the process of their formation. In the ordinary course of nature, flesh and sinew are formed from blood, sinew from the fibrine, due to their kinship, flesh from the coagulation of what is left

d when it is separated from the fibrine. From sinews and flesh again proceeds a viscous oily fluid which glues the flesh to the bones as well as feeding the growth of the bone round the marrow; finally the purest part, consisting of the smoothest and most flexible triangles, and filtering through the bones because of their denseness, flows from the bones and forms drops that

e water the marrow. When the process takes place in this order the normal result is health, when the order is reversed it is disease. When flesh decomposes and the result of the decomposition is discharged back into the veins, the blood in the veins is extensively mixed with air and takes on a variety of colours

and bitternesses, as well as acid and salty qualities, and develops
bile, serum and phlegm of all sorts. These undesirable and
corrupt products first destroy the blood itself, and as they move
in every direction through the veins provide no nourishment        83a
for the body and no longer maintain the natural order of circu-
lation; they conflict with each other because of their mutual
antipathy, they attack any constituent of the body that stands
firm and sticks to its post, and spread destruction and decay.[66]
When the decomposing flesh is of old formation, it resists con-
coction and turns black under long exposure to high tempera-        b
ture; it is eaten right through, turns bitter in consequence and
becomes an attacking agent dangerous to any part of the body
as yet uncorrupted. Sometimes it remains black but acquires
acidity, losing its bitterness which is largely refined away; sometimes it retains its bitterness but an infusion of blood gives it
a reddish tinge which combines with the black to produce a
bilious colour;[67] finally, when the flesh decomposed by the
inflammation is of new formation, yellow colour and bitterness
are combined. The common name of all these products is 'bile',
a name given either by doctors, or by someone capable of          c
looking at many dissimilar things and seeing in them a single
kind which calls for a single name; those that are commonly
recognized as forms of bile each have their own account according to their particular colours.

As to serum, that of the blood is a mild watery part, but that
of black and acid bile, when heat gives the mixture a saline
quality, is a dangerous substance known as 'acid phlegm'. There
is a further substance that results from the decomposition of
young and tender flesh in combination with air. This substance    d
is inflated by air and enveloped by moisture to form bubbles
which are individually too small to be seen, but visible in the
mass, when they form froth, which looks white. The result of
this decomposition of tender flesh in combination with air we
call 'white phlegm'. The watery part of phlegm newly formed
takes the shape of sweat and tears and similar liquids daily       e
excreted.

All these substances, then, are instrumental in producing
disease, when the blood, instead of being replenished by food

and drink in the natural way, receives its mass from the opposite source, contrary to the ordinary course of nature.

When the various kinds of flesh are broken down by disease, but their foundations remain firm, the damage is only half done, for recovery is easy. But when that which binds flesh and bone together is diseased and no longer, keeping itself separate from both flesh and sinews,[68] feeds the bone or binds the flesh to it, but degenerates owing to an unhealthy way of life from its proper oily, smooth, viscous state into a rough, saline, parched condition, then the whole affected substance breaks away from the bones and crumbles into flesh and sinew, and the flesh, falling away from its roots, leaves the sinews bare and full of brine, and falls back into the bloodstream, where it aggravates the disorders already described.

Grievous as these afflictions of the body are, it is still worse when the cause of the trouble is more deep-seated. For example, thickness of the flesh may not allow the bone to breathe adequately. The consequent overheating causes the bone to decay, gangrene sets in and it cannot absorb the fluid which feeds it; by a contrary process bone then dissolves back into fluid, fluid into flesh, flesh into blood, and the type of disorder produced is still more virulent than those already mentioned. But the worst case of all is when the marrow itself becomes diseased because of some deficiency or excess; the most serious and fatal diseases result, as the entire nature of the body is forced to flow in reverse.

## 35. (c) Diseases caused by breath, phlegm and bile; fevers.

Next we must consider a third class of diseases which may be subdivided into those caused by breath, phlegm and bile.

When the lung, which provides the body with breath, is blocked by rheums and its passages choked, the breath does not reach some parts of the body, which putrefy from lack of air; other parts have too great a supply of air which forces its way through the veins and contorts them, dissolves the body and is intercepted by the central barrier of the diaphragm. This

causes a large number of painful disorders, often accompanied
by copious sweating. And often when the flesh disintegrates air
is formed in the body and being unable to escape causes the
same acute pain as if it had been introduced from outside,
particularly when it gathers round the sinews and connected
veins and swells up, pulling backwards the tendons and sinews
attached to them. From the tension so produced the consequent
disorders are called 'tetanus' and 'opisthotonus'.[69] Their cure
is difficult; they are most commonly resolved by supervening
fever.

White phlegm if trapped in the body is dangerous because of    85a
the air in the bubbles; it is less serious if it finds an outlet
from the body, though it disfigures the surface of the body by
producing white patches and similar complaints. Mixed with
black bile it can overlay and confuse the divine circles in the
head; if this happens in sleep the effect is comparatively mild,    b
but an attack in waking hours is more difficult to throw off.
And as the sacred part is affected, the disease is appropriately
called 'sacred'.[70] Acid and saline phlegm is the cause of all
disorders involving a discharge; these have a variety of names
corresponding to the variety of parts affected.

All kinds of inflammation (so called from the burning and
heat which characterizes them) have come to be because of bile.
If the bile finds an outlet it produces various external eruptions;    c
if it is trapped inside it produces many types of fever. The worst
is when it mixes with pure blood and causes disorder in the
fibrine. The fibrine is distributed through the blood to secure a
proportionate consistency and prevent it becoming so liquid
owing to heat that it would run away through the porous
texture of the body or so thick that it would be too sluggish to
circulate in the veins. The natural composition of the fibrine    d
preserves the right balance. And indeed if the fibrine from the
blood of a corpse already cold is collected, the remaining blood
runs out; but if it is left it soon congeals the blood with the
assistance of the surrounding cold. This being the action of
fibrine on blood, bile which was originally blood and now
dissolves back into blood from flesh, on its first entry into the
bloodstream in small quantities, hot and moist, is congealed by

e    the action of the fibrine, and this and its unnatural loss of heat
     cause internal chill and shivering. As the flow of bile increases,
     its heat overcomes the fibrine and boils it up so that it is shaken
     into disorder; and if the bile finally succeeds in getting the upper
     hand, it penetrates to the marrow, burns through the soul's
     mooring-cables and sets it free; but if there is less of it and the
     body resists dissolution, the bile is moistened and expelled from
     the body either through the pores generally, or, if it is forced
86a  through the veins into the upper or lower belly, it is expelled
     from the body like an exile in a civil war in the consequent
     diarrhoea, dysentery and similar disorders.

     A body that has fallen sick owing to excess of fire produces
     continuous heat and fever; excess of air causes daily fever, of
     water fever every third day, water being more sluggish than air
     and fire. Earth, the most sluggish of the four, needs four times
     as long to be purged and every fourth day causes fevers, which
     are hard to shake off.

     ## 36. *Diseases of the soul.*

b    So much for the way in which diseases of the body occur; we
     go on to diseases of the soul caused by bodily condition. It will
     be granted that folly is a disease of the soul, and of folly there
     are two kinds, madness and ignorance. Any affection which
     brings on either must be called a disease and so we must rank
     excessive pleasures and pains as the worst diseases of the soul.
     For when a man enjoys great pleasure, or conversely when he
c    suffers from pain, he is incapable of seeing or hearing anything
     correctly but hurries to grab one thing and avoid another; being
     in a state of frenzy his reasoning power is at this time at its
     lowest. And when the seed in a man's marrow is full and
     overflowing – like a tree producing a disproportionate amount
     of fruit – he gradually acquires many agonies and pleasures
     through his desires and their offspring; being for most of his
d    life in a state of madness induced by the greatest pleasures and
     pains, his soul is deprived of health and judgement by his bodily
     constitution, and he is commonly regarded not as a sick man
     but as deliberately wicked. But the truth is that sexual inconti-

nence is for the most part a disease of the soul caused by the condition of a single substance, which overflows and floods the body because of the porousness of the bones. And indeed it is generally true that it is unjust to blame over-indulgence in pleasure as if wrongdoing were voluntary; no one is bad voluntarily, but a bad man becomes bad because of a pernicious bodily condition and an uneducated upbringing, evils which nobody wants to befall him.

In the same way bodily pains have many bad effects on the soul. Acid and saline phlegm and bitter bilious humours wander about the body, and if they are trapped inside and can get no outlet the vapour that rises from them mixes with the movement of the soul, and the resultant confusion causes a great variety of disorders of different intensity and extent. Relative to which of the three regions of the soul they each attack, they produce different effects: various types first of irritability and depression, next of rashness and timidity, and then of forgetfulness and dullness. Besides, when the constitutions that men with these flaws live under are bad and the way people speak in the city, in private and in public, is bad and they pursue no learning from an early age with the power to cure them, you have the conditions in which all those of us who are bad become so because of two involuntary factors. The responsibility always lies with the parents rather than the offspring, and with those who educate rather than their pupils; but we must all try with all our might by education, by practice and by study to avoid evil and grasp its contrary. That, however, is another story.

## 37. *Proportionality of soul and body.*

It is right and proper that we should next look at the complementary subject, the treatments which cause body and soul to be kept healthy; for there is greater justice in devoting our account to good than to evil. The good, of course, is always beautiful, and the beautiful never lacks measure. A living creature that is to have either quality must therefore be well proportioned. Proportion in minor matters we perceive and understand easily enough, but we often fail to take account of

d  it in matters of major importance. For health and sickness,
virtue and vice, the proportion or disproportion between soul
and body is far the most important factor; yet we pay no
attention to it, and fail to notice that when a strong and powerful soul has too weak and feeble a bodily vehicle, or when the
combination is reversed, the whole creature is without beauty,
because it lacks the most important kind of proportion. When
that proportion is there, on the other hand, you have, for eyes
e  that can see it, the fairest and most desirable of all sights. A
body whose legs are too long, or which has some other part
disproportionately large, is not only ugly but finds that any
coordinated exercise causes it all sorts of trouble, fatigue,
strains and falls owing to its lack of balance. We must expect
the same thing in the combination of soul and body which we
call 'a living thing'. Whenever a soul that is too powerful for
88a  its body becomes very angry, it shakes the whole frame and fills
it with inner disorders; when it enters into intense study and
research the soul breaks down the body; and when it involves
itself in teaching and verbal contests, public or private, through
the consequent quarrels and contentiousness, the soul fires up
and shakes the body, bringing on rheums that deceive most
so-called physicians into citing causes opposite to the true. On
the other hand, when a large body is joined to a small and
b  intellectually feeble soul for which it is too big, of the two
natural human appetites, the body's for food and the most
divine part's for wisdom, the motions of the stronger part
prevail and increase the power of their own kind, while they
make the soul dull, slow to learn and forgetful, and bring about
the worst of diseases, ignorance. There is one safeguard against
both dangers, which is to avoid exercising either body or soul
without the other, and thus preserve an equal and healthy
c  balance between them. So anyone engaged in mathematics or
any other strenuous intellectual pursuit should also exercise his
body and take part in physical training; while the man who
devotes himself to physical fitness must correspondingly provide due motions for the soul by applying himself to the arts
and all manner of philosophy. Only so can either rightly be
called at once 'beautiful and good'.[71]

## 38. *Bodily health and the avoidance of drugs.*

The parts of the body should be looked after on the same
principles, imitating the pattern of the universe. For the body     d
is heated and cooled internally by what enters it and dried and
moistened by its external environment, and is subject to the
disturbances consequent on both processes. If a man yields his
body passively to them they overcome it and destroy it; but if
he imitates what we have called the nurse and foster-mother of
the universe,[72] he will never, if possible, allow his body to
remain passively at rest, but will keep it in motion and by
producing tremors throughout the whole body defend himself     e
in accordance with nature against the internal and external
motions. By such moderate shaking he can reduce to order and
system the affections and parts that wander through the body
according to their affinities, in the same way that we have
described in speaking of the universe; and so he will not leave
foe ranged by foe to generate war and disease in the body, but
friend by friend to produce health. Among movements, the best     89a
is the movement produced in oneself by oneself – for it is most
nearly akin to the movement of intelligence and of the universe;
next is movement produced in us by another; worst of all is
movement caused by outside agents in parts of the body while
the body itself remains passive and inert. So the best way of
purging and toning up the body is by exercise; next is the
swaying of a ship or the motion of any vehicle that does not
cause fatigue; last, and for use in extreme necessity, though not     b
otherwise if we have any sense, is purging by medicine and
drugs. Indeed, unless the danger is grave, diseases should not
be irritated by the use of drugs. For the entire structure of
diseases is in a certain way similar to the nature of living beings.
Living beings are so constituted that there is a set period of life
for the entire kind; and for each individual born there is (barring     c
inevitable accidents) an allotted life-span, as its triangles are
from the first constituted to last for a certain time, beyond
which its life cannot be prolonged. The same is true of the
structure of diseases; and if their allotted period is interfered
with by the use of drugs, they are commonly rendered more

serious or more frequent. All kinds of diseases therefore should,
d  so far as leisure permits, be attended to by a proper regime of
life, and stubborn complaints should not be irritated by drugs.

### 39. Health of the soul.

So much then for the living creature as a whole and for its
bodily part, and for the way in which a man can educate himself
and by that education be enabled to lead a rational life. And,
for this reason, I believe that we should first and with the
greatest possible care prepare that part which is to educate us,
e  so that it will be the finest and best possible educator. To deal
with this subject in detail would be a considerable task in itself;
but, treating it as a side issue, we shall not be far wrong if we
confine ourselves to the next observations, which follow on
from our previous argument. As we have said more than once,
there are housed in us three distinct forms of soul, each having
its own motions. Accordingly we may now say, very briefly,
that any of these forms that lives in idleness and fails to exercise
its own proper motions is bound to become very feeble, while
any that exercises them will become very strong; hence we must
90a  take care that these motions are properly proportioned to each
other. We should think of the most authoritative part of our
soul as a guardian spirit given to each of us by god, living in
the summit of the body, which can properly be said to lift us
from the earth towards our home in heaven, as if we were a
heavenly and not an earthbound plant. For where the soul first
grew into being, from there our divine part attaches us by the
head to heaven, like a plant by its roots, and keeps our body
b  upright. If therefore a man's attention and effort have been
centred on appetite and ambition, all his opinions are bound to
have become mortal, and he can hardly fail, in so far as it is
possible, to become entirely mortal, as it is his mortal part that
he has increased. But a man who has given his heart to learning
and true wisdom and exercised that part of himself is surely
c  bound, if he attains to truth, to have immortal and divine
thoughts, and cannot fail to participate in immortality as fully
as is possible for human nature; and because he has always

looked after the divine element in himself and kept his guardian
spirit in good order he, above all men, must be happy. There is
of course only one way to look after anything and that is to
give it its proper nourishment and motions. And the motions
that are akin to the divine in us are the thoughts and revolutions   d
of the universe. We should each therefore attend to these
motions and by learning thoroughly about the harmonies and
revolutions of the universe repair the damage done to the circuits in our head in connection with our coming into being,
and so restore our understanding, in accordance with its original nature, to its likeness with the object of understanding.
When that is done we shall have achieved the goal set us by the
gods, the life that is best for this present time and for all time
to come.

## 40. Sexual reproduction; creation of women, birds, animals, reptiles and fish.

I think we may now claim that our original assignment – to tell   e
the story of the universe till the coming into being of man – is
pretty well complete. The way the other animals have come
into being can be dealt with quite shortly, and there is no need
to say much about it; for when it comes to accounts of these
matters someone speaking in this manner will seem more
measured to himself. So let this kind of account be presented
as follows.

The men of the first generation who lived cowardly or unjust
lives were, in accordance with the likely account, reborn in the
second generation as women; and it was therefore at that point   91a
of time that the gods produced sexual desire, constructing in us
and in women a living creature itself endowed with soul. This
is how they did it. There is a passage for drinking by which
what we drink makes its way through the lung into the kidneys
and thence to the bladder from which it is expelled by air
pressure. From this passage they pierced a hole into the column
of marrow which extends from the head down through the
neck along the spine and which we have already referred to as   b
'seed'; this marrow, being endowed with soul and finding an

outlet, caused in that place a vital appetite for emission, and thereby the love of reproduction. So a man's genitals are naturally disobedient and self-willed, like an animal that will not listen to reason, and will do anything in their mad lust for possession. Much the same is true, and for the same reasons,

c of the so-called 'matrix' or 'womb' in women, which is a living being within them which desires to bear children. And if it is left fruitless long beyond the normal time, it causes extreme unrest, strays in the body in every direction, blocks the channels of the breath and causes in consequence acute distress and

d disorders of all kinds. This goes on until the woman's desire and the man's love meet and pick the fruit from the tree, as it were, sowing the plough-land of the womb with living beings as yet unformed and too small to be seen. They cause the creatures to take shape and nourish them within until they complete their generation by bringing them into the light of day as complete living creatures.

That is how women and the female sex generally came into being. The race of birds was produced by a process of transformation, whereby feathers grew instead of hair, from harmless, empty-headed men, who were interested in the heavens but

e were silly enough to think that the most certain astronomical demonstrations proceed through observation. Wild land animals have come from men who made no use of philosophy and never in any way considered the nature of the heavens because they had ceased to use the circles in the head and followed the leadership of the parts of the soul in the breast. Because of these practices their fore-limbs and heads were drawn by natural affinity to the earth, and their fore-limbs supported on it, while their skulls were elongated into various shapes according to the

92a particular way in which each man's circles had been crushed through lack of use. And the reason why some have four feet and others many was that the stupider they were the more supports god gave them, to drag them down more closely to the earth. And as for the most foolish of the land animals, whose whole bodies lie stretched on the earth, since they had no further need of feet, the god created them footless and

b wriggling on the ground. But the most unintelligent and ignorant of all has come into being as the fourth kind of creature that lives in water. Their souls were hopelessly mired in every kind of error, and so their makers thought them unfit to breathe pure clean air, and made them inhale water, into whose turbid depths they plunged them. That is the origin of fish, shell-fish and everything else that lives in water; they live in the depths as a punishment for the depth of their stupidity. These are the principles on which living creatures change and have always changed into each other, the transformation depending on the loss or gain of understanding or folly.

## 41. *Conclusion.*

Let us now declare that our account of the universe has reached its end. For our world has received mortal and immortal living beings and has been completed in this way: as a visible living creature containing all creatures that are visible, a perceptible god which is an image of the intelligible, as the greatest and best, the most beautiful and most complete, this heaven, being one and unique in kind, has come into being.

# CRITIAS

## 1. *Introductory conversation.*

TIMAEUS: How glad I am, Socrates, to have brought my story safely to an end, and how pleased to get some rest after my long journey. I pray to the god who came into being in words just now, though in fact he came into being a long time ago, that we may safely retain all that has been said with measure, but pay suitable penalty for any false notes we have involuntarily struck. And the correct penalty for the one who plays out of tune is to make him play in tune. I pray therefore that god may grant us knowledge, the most effective and best of all medicines, so that all we say in future about the coming into being of gods may be correct; and with that prayer I pass on the job of giving the next speech to Critias, as agreed.

CRITIAS: And I accept it, Timaeus. But I must make the same plea that you made at the beginning, and ask for indulgence because of the magnitude of my theme. Indeed I think the nature of my subject gives me an even greater claim to it. I know that what I am going to ask will seem excessive and unnecessarily embarrassing, but ask I must. No one in his senses could challenge the excellence of the account you have given: it remains for me to try to show that my subject is a more difficult one and therefore calls for greater indulgence. For it is easier, Timaeus, to give a satisfactory impression when talking to men about the gods than when talking among ourselves about mortals. For inexperience and ignorance of a subject in your audience make it very easy to handle if you are to talk about it; and we know how ignorant we are about the gods. Follow me a bit further along this way so that my meaning may be clearer.

c   All the things we say are inevitably imitation and likeness. So let us consider the relative degree of severity with which we judge the adequacy of the production of images by artists of divine and of human objects. We see that we are satisfied if the artist can produce quite an elementary likeness of earth, mountains, rivers and woods, and of the sky and stars and planets; besides, because of our lack of clear knowledge of such

d   matters, we don't subject his pictures to any searching criticism, being content with an imprecise and deceptive sketch. But if anyone tries to make a likeness of the human body, we are, because of our familiarity with it, quick to notice faults and criticize severely any failure to produce a perfect likeness. We should recognize that the same is true of words. We are content with faint likenesses when their subjects are celestial and divine, but we criticize narrowly when they are mortal and human. So

e   in what will now be said on the spur of the moment, you should make allowances if my narrative is not always entirely appropriate; for you must understand that it is far from easy to

108a produce a likeness of human affairs that will meet with approval. It is to remind you of this and to ask for a still greater degree of indulgence for what I am going to say, Socrates, that I have started with this long introduction. If you think the favour I'm asking is justified, please grant it.

    SOCRATES: Of course we will, Critias; and Hermocrates may assume that we will grant the same indulgence to him. For in a

b   little while, when it is his turn to speak, he will obviously make the same request as you have. So, in order that he will not feel the need to make the same introduction, but rather produce another of his own, let him assume the request granted. But I warn you, my dear Critias, of the mind of the audience: the poet who preceded you has made a wonderfully favourable impression,[1] so you will need a great deal of allowance made for you if you are to take over from him.

    HERMOCRATES: That warning applies to me as much as to

c   him, Socrates. But 'faint-hearted men never yet set up a trophy',[2] Critias; you must tackle your narrative like a man, and call on Pan and the Muses for their help in showing the virtues of your fellow-citizens of old and singing their praises.

CRITIAS: My dear Hermocrates, you are still brave because you are in the rear rank with someone to shelter you. But you will find out soon enough from experience what kind of thing   d we are dealing with. Meanwhile I must follow your encouraging advice and call on the gods, adding the goddess Memory in particular to those you have mentioned. For my whole narrative depends largely on her. I'm sure my audience will think I have discharged my task with reasonable credit if I can remember adequately and repeat the story which the priests told Solon and he brought home with him. To it I must now proceed without further delay.

## 2. *Time-scale and catastrophe.*

We must first remind ourselves that in all nine thousand years   e have elapsed, according to the records, since the war occurred between those who lived outside and all those who lived inside the Pillars of Heracles. This is the war whose course I am to trace. It was said that the leadership and conduct of the entire war were on the one side in the hands of our city, on the other in the hands of the kings of Atlantis. At the time, as we said, Atlantis was an island larger than Libya and Asia put together, though it was subsequently overwhelmed by earthquakes and is the source of the impenetrable mud which prevents the free   109a passage of those who sail out of the straits into the open sea.[3] The course of our narrative as it unfolds will give particulars about the various barbarian and Greek nations of the day; but we must begin with an account of the resources and consti-tutions of the Athenians and their antagonists in the war, giving precedence to the Athenians.

Once upon a time the gods divided up the whole Earth   b between them according to its regions – not in the course of a quarrel; for it would be quite wrong to think that the gods do not know what is appropriate to them, or that, knowing it, they would want to annex what properly belongs to others. Each gladly received his just allocation, and settled his terri-tories; and having done so they proceeded to look after us, their creatures and children, as shepherds look after their flocks.

c   They did not use physical means of control, like shepherds who
    direct their flock with blows, but directed the creature from the
    stern where it is most easily turned; using persuasion as a
    steersman does the helm, they took hold of the soul as they saw
    fit and so led and governed the whole mortal creature. The
    various gods, then, administered the various regions which had
    been allotted to them. But Hephaestus and Athena, who having
    the same father shared a common nature and pursued the same
    ends in their love of knowledge and craft, were allotted this

d   land of ours as their joint sphere and as a suitable and natural
    home for excellence and wisdom. They produced a native race
    of good men and gave them suitable political arrangements.
    Their names have been preserved but what they did has been
    forgotten because of the destruction of their successors and the
    long lapse of time. For, as we said before,[4] the survivors of this
    destruction were an unlettered mountain race who had just
    heard the names of the rulers of the land but knew little of their

e   achievements. They were glad enough to give their names to
    their own children, but they knew nothing of the virtues and
    institutions of their predecessors, except for a few hazy reports;

110a for many generations they and their children were short of bare
    necessities, and their minds and conversations were focused on
    providing for them, to the neglect of earlier history and tra-
    dition. For the study of myths and research into ancient history
    visit cities only in the company of leisure, when they see that
    some people have been provided with the necessities of life.[5]
    That is how the names but not the achievements of these early
    generations came to be preserved. My evidence is this: that

b   Cecrops, Erechtheus, Erichthonius, Erysichthon and most of
    the other names recorded before Theseus, occurred, according
    to Solon, in the narrative of the priests about this war; and the
    same is true of the women's names. What is more, as men and
    women in those days both took part in military exercises, so
    the figure and image of the Goddess, following this custom,
    was in full armour, as a sign that whenever animals herd

c   together, male and female, it is natural for each kind in its
    entirety to be able to practise together the excellence appropri-
    ate to it.[6]

## 3. Prehistoric Athens: the land, the people and their institutions.

In those days there lived in this country classes of citizens concerned with manufacture and agriculture. The military class lived apart, having been from the beginning separated from the others by godlike men. They were provided with what was necessary for their maintenance and training, they had no private property but regarded their possessions as common to all,   d they did not look to the rest of the citizens for anything beyond their basic maintenance; in fact they followed in all things the regime we laid down yesterday when we were talking about our hypothetical guards.[7] Moreover, what used to be said about our territory is true and plausible enough; for in those days its boundaries were drawn at the Isthmus, and on the mainland   e side at the Cithaeron and Parnes ranges coming down to the sea between Oropus on the right and the Asopus river on the left. And the soil was said to be more fertile than any other and therefore our country could maintain a large army exempt from the calls of agricultural labour. As evidence of this fertility we can point to the fact that the remnant of it still left is a match for any soil in the world for the variety of its harvests and the   111a rich pasture it provides for all kinds of animals. And in those days quantity matched quality. What proof then can we offer that it is fair to call it now a mere remnant of what it once was? It runs out like a long peninsula from the mainland into the sea, and the sea basin round it is very deep. So the result of the many great floods that have taken place in the last nine thousand years (the time that has elapsed since then) is that the soil washed away from the high land in these periodical catas-   b trophes forms no alluvial deposit of consequence as in other places, but is carried out and lost in the deeps. As with little islands, you are left with something now which compared to what was is rather like the skeleton of a body wasted by disease; the rich, soft soil has all run away leaving the land nothing but clean bone. But in those days the damage had not taken place, the hills had high crests, the so-called 'rocky plains' were   c covered with rich soil, and the mountains were covered by thick woods, of which there are some traces today. For some mountains which today will only support bees produced not so long ago trees which when cut provided roof beams for huge buildings whose roofs are still standing. And there were a lot of tall cultivated trees which bore unlimited quantities of fodder

d for beasts. The soil benefited from an annual rainfall from Zeus which did not run to waste off the bare earth as it does today, but was absorbed in large quantities and stored in retentive layers of clay, so that what was soaked up by the higher regions flowed downwards into the valleys and appeared everywhere in a multitude of rivers and springs. And the shrines which still survive at these former springs are proof of the truth of our present account of the country.

e      This, then, was the general nature of the country, and it was cultivated with the skill you would expect from a class of genuine full-time agriculturalists with good natural talents and high standards, who had an excellent soil, an abundant water supply and a well-balanced climate. The layout of the city in

112a those days was as follows. The Acropolis was different from what it is now. Today it is quite bare of soil which was all washed away in one appalling night of flood, by a combination of earthquakes and the third terrible deluge before that of Deucalion.[8] Prior to that, in earlier days, it extended to the Eridanus and Ilisus, it included the Pnyx and was bounded on the opposite side by the Lycabettus; it was covered with soil

b and for the most part level. Outside, on its immediate slopes, lived the craftsmen and the agricultural workers who were farming in the neighbourhood. Higher up the military class lived by itself round the temple of Athena and Hephaestus, surrounded by a single wall like the garden of a single house. On the northern side they built their common dwelling-houses

c and winter mess-rooms, and everything else required by the communal life of themselves and the priests. They had no gold or silver, and never used these for any purpose, but aimed at a balance between extravagance and meanness in the houses they built, in which they and their descendants grew old and which they handed on unchanged to succeeding generations who resembled themselves. In the summer they abandoned their gardens and gymnasia and mess-rooms and used the southern side of the Acropolis instead. There was a single spring in the d area of the present Acropolis, which was subsequently choked by the earthquakes and survives in only a few small trickles in the vicinity; in those days there was an ample supply of good water both in winter and summer. This was how they lived; and they acted as guards of their own citizens, and were voluntarily recognized as leaders of the rest of Greece. They kept the number of those of military age, men and women, so far as e possible, always constant at about twenty thousand.

This then was the sort of people they were and this the way in which they administered justly their own affairs and those of Greece; their reputation and name stood higher than any other in Europe and Asia for their physical beauty and total virtue of soul. I will now go on to reveal to you, as friends,[9] if I can still remember what I was told when I was a child, the nature and origin of their antagonists in the war.

## 4. Atlantis. (a) Explanation of nomenclature.

Before I begin, a brief word of explanation, in case you are 113a surprised at hearing foreigners so often referred to by Greek names. The reason is this. Solon intended to use the story in his own poem. And when, on inquiring about the significance of the names, he learned that those Egyptians who first wrote them down had translated them into their own language, he b went through the reverse process, and as he learned the meaning of a name wrote it in Greek. My grandfather had his manuscript, which is now in my possession, and I studied it often as a child. So if you hear names like those we use here, don't be surprised; I have given you the reason. The story is a long one and it begins like this.

## 4. (b) Origins: Poseidon and Cleito, their descendants, the natural resources of the island.

We have already mentioned how the gods distributed the whole earth between them in larger or smaller shares and then c established shrines and sacrifices for themselves. Poseidon's share was the island of Atlantis and he settled the children borne to him by a mortal woman in a district of it which I will now describe. From the sea extending across the middle of the whole island[10] there was a plain, said to the most beautiful and fertile of all plains, and near the middle of this plain about fifty stades[11] inland a hill of no great size. Here there lived one of

d  the original earth-born inhabitants called Evenor, with his wife Leucippe. They had an only child, a daughter called Cleito. She was just of marriageable age when her father and mother died, and Poseidon was attracted by her and had intercourse with her, and he fortified the hill where she lived by enclosing it with concentric rings, alternately of sea and land, and of varying sizes, two rings of land and three of sea, which from the centre of the island he turned as if with a lathe and chisel so that they

e  were at every point equidistant from each other, thereby making the hill inaccessible to man (for there were still no ships or sailing in those days). Poseidon easily set in order the central island, in the manner one expects of a god; he made two springs flow, one hot and one of cold water, and caused the earth to grow abundant produce of every kind. He begot five pairs of male twins, brought them up, and divided the island of Atlantis into ten parts which he distributed between them. He allotted

114a  the elder of the eldest pair of twins his mother's home district and the land surrounding it, the biggest and best allocation, and made him king over the others; the others he made governors, each of a populous and large territory. He gave them all names. The eldest, the king, he gave a name from which the

b  whole island and surrounding ocean took their designation of 'Atlantic', deriving it from Atlas the first king. His twin, to whom was allocated the furthest part of the island towards the Pillars of Heracles and facing the district now called Gadira,[12] was called in Greek Eumelus but in his own language Gadirus, which is presumably the origin of the present name. Of the second pair he called one Ampheres and the other Euaemon.

c  The elder of the third pair was called Mneseus, the younger Autochthon, the elder of the fourth Elasippus, the younger Mestor; the name given to the elder of the firth pair was Azaes, to the younger Diaprepes. They and their descendants for many generations governed their own territories and many other islands in the ocean and, as has already been said, also controlled the populations this side of the straits as far as Egypt and Tyrrhenia. Atlas had a long and distinguished line of descendants, eldest son succeeding eldest son and maintaining the succession unbroken for many generations; their wealth was greater than that possessed by any previous dynasty of kings or likely to be accumulated by any later, and both in the city and countryside they were provided with everything they could require. Because of the extent of their power they received many imports, but for most of their needs the island itself provided. It had mineral resources from which were mined both solid materials and metals,[13] including one metal which survives today only in name, but was then mined in quantities in a number of localities in the island, orichalc,[14] in those days the most valuable metal except gold. The island offered a plentiful supply of timber for structural purposes, and fed every kind of animal domesticated and wild, among them numerous elephants. For there was plenty of grazing for this largest and most voracious of beasts, as well as for all creatures whose habitat is marsh, swamp and river, mountain or plain. Besides all this, the earth bore freely all the aromatic substances it bears today, roots, herbs, bushes and gums exuded by flowers or fruit. There were cultivated crops, cereals which provide our staple diet, and pulse (to use its generic name) which we need in addition to feed us; there were the fruits of trees, hard to store but providing the drink and food and oil which give us pleasure and relaxation and which we serve after supper as a welcome refreshment to the weary when appetite is satisfied – all these were produced by that sacred island, then still beneath the sun, in wonderful quality and profusion. This then was the island's natural endowment, and the inhabitants proceeded to build temples, palaces, harbours and docks, and set in order the country as a whole in the following manner.

### 4. (c) The city and the buildings.[15]

Their first work was to bridge the rings of water round their mother's original home, so forming a road to and from their palace. This palace they proceeded to build at once in the place where the god and their ancestors had lived, and each successive

d  king added to its beauties, doing his best to surpass his predecessors, until they had made a residence whose size and beauty were astonishing to see. They began by digging a canal three hundred feet wide, a hundred feet deep and fifty stades long from the sea to the outermost ring, thus making it accessible from the sea like a harbour; and they made the entrance to it

e  large enough to admit the largest ships. At the bridges they made channels through the rings of land which separated those of water, large enough to admit the passage of a single trireme, and roofed over to make an underground tunnel; for the rims of the rings were of some height above sea-level. The largest of the rings, to which there was access from the sea, was three stades in breadth and the ring of land within it the same. Of the second pair the ring of water was two stades in breadth, and the ring of land again equal to it, while the ring of water running immediately round the central island was a stade

116a  across. The diameter of the island on which the palace was situated was five stades. It and the rings and the bridges (which were a hundred feet broad) were enclosed by a stone wall all around, with towers and gates guarding the bridges on either side where they crossed the water. The stone for them, some

b  white, some black and the other red, they cut out of the central island and the outer and inner rings of land, and in the process excavated pairs of hollow docks with roofs of rock. Some of their buildings were of a single colour, in others they mixed different coloured stone to divert the eye and afford them appropriate pleasure. And they covered the whole circuit of the outermost wall with bronze, as if applying a varnish, and they

c  fused tin over the inner wall and orichalc gleaming like fire over the wall of the acropolis itself.

The construction of the palace within the acropolis was as follows. In the centre was a shrine sacred to Poseidon and

Cleito, surrounded by a golden wall through which entry was forbidden, as it was the place where the family of the ten kings was conceived and begotten; and there year by year seasonal offerings were made from the ten provinces to each one of them. There was a temple of Poseidon himself, a stade in length, three hundred feet wide and proportionate in height, though somewhat barbarian in appearance. The outside of it was covered all over with silver, except for the figures on the pediment which were covered with gold. Inside, the roof was ivory picked out with gold, silver and orichalc, and all the walls, pillars and floor were covered with orichalc. It contained gold statues of the god standing in a chariot drawn by six winged horses, so tall that his head touched the roof, and round him, riding on dolphins, a hundred Nereids (that being the accepted number of them at the time), as well as many other statues dedicated by private persons. Round the temple were gold statues of all the wives and descendants of the ten kings, and many other large votive offerings of kings and private persons belonging to the city and its dominions. There was an altar of a size and workmanship to match that of the building and a palace equally worthy of the greatness of the empire and the magnificence of its temples. The two springs, cold and hot, provided an unlimited supply of water for appropriate purposes, remarkable for its agreeable quality and excellence; and this they made available by surrounding it with suitable buildings and plantations, leading some of it into basins in the open air and some of it into covered hot baths for winter use. Here separate accommodation was provided for royalty and for commoners, and, again, for women, for horses and for other beasts of burden, appropriately equipped in each case. The outflow they led into the grove of Poseidon, which (because of the goodness of the soil) was full of trees of marvellous beauty and height, and also channelled it to the outer ring-islands by aqueducts at the bridges. On each of these ring-islands they had built many temples for different gods, and many gardens and areas for exercise, some for men and some for horses. In particular, in the middle of the larger island there was a special course reserved for horse-racing; its width was a stade and its length

that of a complete circuit of the island. Round it on both sides
d were barracks for the main body of the king's personal guard.
A more select group of the more trustworthy were stationed
on the smaller island ring nearer the citadel, and the most
trustworthy of all had quarters assigned to them in the citadel
and were attached to the king's person.

Finally, there were dockyards full of triremes and their equipment, all in good shape.

So much then for the arrangement of the royal residence and
its environs. Beyond the three outer harbours there was a wall,
e beginning at the sea and running right round in a circle, at a
uniform distance of fifty stades from the largest ring and harbour and returning on itself at the mouth of the canal to the
sea. This wall was densely built up all around with houses and
the canal and large harbour were crowded with vast numbers
of merchant ships from all quarters, from which rose a constant
din of shouting and noise day and night.

## 4. (d) The rest of the island.[16]

I have given you a pretty complete account of what was told
118a me about the city and its original buildings; I must now try to
recall the nature and organization of the rest of the country. To
begin with, the region as a whole was said to be high above the
level of the sea, from which it rose precipitously; the city was
surrounded by a uniformly flat plain, which was in turn
enclosed by mountains which came right down to the sea. This
plain was rectangular in shape, measuring three thousand stades
in length and at its midpoint two thousand stades in breadth
b from the coast. This whole area of the island faced south, and
was sheltered from the north winds. The mountains which
surrounded it were celebrated as being more numerous, higher
and more beautiful than any which exist today; and in them
were numerous villages and a wealthy population, as well as
rivers and lakes and meadows, which provided ample pasture
for all kinds of domesticated and wild animals, and a plentiful
variety of woodland to supply abundant timber for every kind
of manufacture.

Over a long period of time the work of a number of kings c
had effected certain modifications in the natural features of the
plain. It was naturally a long, regular rectangle; and any defects
in its shape were corrected by means of a ditch dug around it.
The depth and breadth and length of this may sound incredible
for an artificial structure when compared with others of a
similar kind, but I must give them as I heard them. The depth
was a hundred feet, the width at every point a stade, and the
length, since it was dug right around the plain, was ten thousand d
stades.[17] The rivers which flowed down from the mountains
emptied into it, and it made a complete circuit of the plain,
running round to the city from both directions, and there discharged into the sea.[18] Channels about a hundred feet broad
were cut from the ditch's landward limb straight across the
plain, at a distance of a hundred stades from each other, till
they ran into it on its seaward side. They cut cross channels
between them and also to the city, and used the whole complex e
to float timber down from the mountains and transport
seasonal produce by boat. They had two harvests a year, a
winter one for which they relied on rainfall and a summer one
for which the channels, fed by the rivers, provided irrigation.

## 4. (e) Military service.

The distribution of manpower was as follows: each allotment
of land was under obligation to furnish one male leader of a 119a
military detachment. Each allotment was ten square stades in
size and there were in all 60,000 allotments; there was said to
be an unlimited supply of men in the mountains and other parts
of the country and they were assigned by district and village to
all the leaders of the allotments. The leader was bound to
provide a sixth part of the equipment of a war chariot, up to a
total complement of 10,000, with two horses and riders; and
in addition a pair of horses without a chariot, a combatant b
with light shield who descends from the chariot to fight, the
charioteer who drives the horses and sits behind a combatant
who fights from the chariot,[19] two hoplites, two archers and
two slingers, three light-armed stone-throwers and three javelin

men, and four sailors as part of the complement of twelve hundred ships. Such were the military dispositions of the royal city; those of the other nine varied in detail and it would take too long to describe them.

## 4. (f) Political and legal authority.

c   Their arrangements for the distribution of authority and office were as follows. Each of the ten kings had absolute power, in his own region and city, over persons and in general over laws, and could punish or execute at will. But the distribution of power between them and their mutual relations were governed by the injunctions of Poseidon, enshrined in the law and d   engraved by the first kings on an orichalc pillar in the temple of Poseidon in the middle of the island. Here they assembled alternately every fifth and sixth year (thereby showing equal respect to both odd and even numbers), consulted on matters of mutual interest and inquired into and gave judgement on any wrong committed by any of them. And before any prospective judgement they exchanged mutual pledges in the following ceremony. There were in the temple of Poseidon bulls roaming at large. The ten kings, after praying to the god that they e   might secure a sacrifice that would please him, entered alone by themselves and started a hunt for a bull, using clubs and nooses but no metal weapon; and when they caught him they cut his throat over the top of the pillar so that the blood flowed over the inscription. And on the pillar there was engraved, in addition to the laws, an oath invoking awful curses on those 120a who disobeyed it. When they had finished the ritual of sacrifice and were consecrating the limbs of the bull, they mixed a bowl of wine and dropped in a clot of blood for each of them, before cleansing the pillar and burning the rest of the blood. After this they drew wine from the bowl in golden cups, poured a libation over the fire and swore an oath to give judgement in accordance with the laws written on the pillar, to punish any past offences, never knowingly in future to transgress what was written, b   and finally neither to give nor obey orders unless they were in accordance with the laws of their father. Each one of them swore this oath on his own behalf and that of his descendants, and after drinking dedicated his cup to the god's temple. There followed an interval for supper and necessary business, and then when darkness fell and the sacrificial fire had died down they all put on the most splendid dark blue ceremonial robes and sat on the ground by the embers of the sacrificial fire, in the dark, all glimmer of fire in the sanctuary being extinguished. c And thus they gave and submitted to judgement on any complaints of wrong made against them; and afterwards, when it was light, wrote the terms of the judgement on gold plates which they dedicated together with their robes as a record. And among many other special laws governing the privileges of the kings the most important were that they should never make war on each other, but come to each other's help if any of them were threatened with a dissolution of the power of the royal house in his state; in that case, they should follow the custom d of their predecessors and consult mutually about policy for war and other matters, recognizing the suzerainty of the House of Atlas. But the king of that house should have no authority to put any of his fellows to death without the consent of a majority of the ten.


## 5. Degeneration and punishment.

This was the nature and extent of the power which existed then in those parts of the world and which god brought to attack our country. His reason, so the story goes, was this. For many e generations, so long as the divine element in their nature survived, they obeyed the laws and loved the divine to which they were akin. They maintained thoughts that were true and in every way lofty, treating the vagaries of fortune and one another with wisdom and forbearance, as they reckoned that qualities of character were far more important than their present prosperity. So they bore the burden, as it were, of their wealth and 121a possessions lightly, and their wealth did not make them drunk with conceit and so lose their self-control and falter, but they saw soberly and clearly that all these things flourish only on a soil of common goodwill and virtue, and if pursued too eagerly and overvalued destroy themselves and virtue with them. So long as these principles and their divine nature remained unimpaired the prosperity which we have described continued to grow.

b But when the divine portion in them became weakened by frequent admixture of a large quantity of mortal stock, and their human traits became predominant, they ceased to be able to carry their prosperity with moderation. To the perceptive eye they appeared shameful, since they were destroying the finest of their most precious possessions, but to those whose judgement of true happiness is defective they seemed, in their pursuit of unbridled ambition and power, to be supremely fine and blessed. And the god of gods, Zeus, who reigns by law, and whose eye can see such things, when he perceived the wretched state of this admirable stock decided to punish them

c and reduce them to order by discipline.

He accordingly summoned all the gods to his own most glorious abode, which stands at the centre of the entire cosmos and looks out over the whole realm of becoming, and when he had assembled them he spoke . . .

# Notes

## TIMAEUS

1. For more information on Critias and the other characters, see D. Nails, *The People of Plato: A Prosopography of Plato and Other Socratics* (Indianapolis, 2002). (TJ)

2. The reference is to the annual festival of Athena. (TJ)

3. An annual festival at which male children were entered into the tribe (*phratria*). (TJ)

4. In classical Greece, Egypt, or part of it, was sometimes considered part of Asia, cf. Herodotus, *Histories*, Book 2. (TJ)

5. That is, the Strait of Gibraltar. (TJ)

6. A region of central Italy. (TJ)

7. Possibly a reference to Solon's laws which conferred citizenship on serfs (*thêtes*) and exiles. (TJ)

8. 'Living being' here translates *zôion*, which might also here, and in similar contexts, be rendered as 'animal'. We would then have to think of plants as animals too since they are referred to as *zôia* (77b). Such a conception might be defended on the grounds that Timaeus thinks that plants have perception of pleasure and pain, where having perception is, if we follow Aristotle, the hallmark of animals (cf. D. Sedley, *Creationism and Its Critics in Antiquity*, ch. 4, n. 2). However, Timaeus explicitly defends calling plants *zôia*, not on the basis of their having perception, but because 'everything that has life [*to zên*] has every right to be called a living thing [*zôion*]' (77b). (TJ)

9. The general algebraic formula is

   if a:b::b:c then c:b::b:a and b:a::c:b

10. The seven motions are: uniform circular motion in the same place, mentioned here, up and down, backwards and forwards, right and left.

11.

FIGURE 7  The armillary sphere (the Mansell Collection).

12.  Cornford (*Cosmology*, p. 61) suggests:
We may set out the full scheme of the soul's composition as
follows:

|  | *First Mixture* |  |  | *Final Mixture* |
|---|---|---|---|---|
| Indivisible Being | | Intermediate | | |
| Divisible Being | } | Being | | |
| | | | | |
| Indivisible Sameness | | Intermediate | | |
| Divisible Sameness | } | Sameness | } | Soul |
| | | | | |
| Indivisible Difference | | Intermediate | | |
| Divisible Difference | } | Difference | | |

In 35a4, read *au peri* after *phuseôs* with Cornford.

13. The series 1, 2, 3, 4, 9, 8, 27, which, as ancient commentators pointed out, can be arranged in the following diagram:

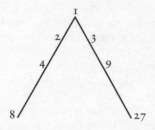

In this $4 = 2^2$ and $8 = 2^3$, $9 = 3^2$ and $27 = 3^3$. In Plato's description the numbers measure off corresponding lengths on a single strip of soul-stuff. 4 and 9, 8 and 27 are square and cube numbers which are thought of as two-dimensional and three-dimensional, planes and solids. 'The reason for stopping at the cube is that the cube symbolizes body in three dimensions' (Cornford, *Cosmology*, p. 68).

14. Plato now treats the intervals which he has marked out on his soul-stuff as if they defined a musical scale.

15. For a detailed explanation of this very compressed description, see Cornford, *Cosmology*, pp. 80 ff. All circles share the movement of the same (the daily rotation of the fixed stars), but the seven circles or bands of the different each have an additional motion in a contrary sense, briefly referred to here. The three which revolve at the same speed, which may be regarded as the standard speed of the different, are the Sun, Venus and Mercury; the remaining four move at speeds differing from each other and that of the three. Plato's expression is made still more obscure because he has not yet mentioned the planets to whose movements the sentence refers. The basic principle in his scheme is that of explaining the motions of the Sun, Moon and planets as the combined result of two or more motions.

16. Lee, following Cornford, has 'shrine for the eternal gods'. The main reason for the reading I have adopted is that Timaeus clearly has in mind the likeness of the creation to the paradigm: so he goes on to say that the father wanted to make the world 'still more like its pattern'. Cornford's rendition also suffers from the problem that we have not yet been told that the universe and

in particular the heavenly bodies are gods, so the reference of 'eternal gods' remains obscure to the reader at this point. The main objection to my reading is that it implies that the forms are gods, which is something Timaeus does not say. However, it is plausible to think that he would call the particular forms that provide the paradigm for the world gods since it is an eternal living being that contains all the other living beings within it. (TJ)

17. To understand the contrast, the reader needs to bear in mind that for the Greeks 'number' implies 'plurality'; so 'one' is not a number. (TJ)

18. The change to the present tense may simply be for the rhetorical purpose of vividness here, but in a passage that is concerned with how we should talk about time it seems right to reflect the change of tense in the translation. (TJ)

19. There has been much discussion of what is meant by this 'power of motion contrary to his'; see Cornford, *Cosmology*, p. 106, A. E. Taylor, *A Commentary on Plato's 'Timaeus'*, p. 196, A. Gregory, *Plato's Philosophy of Science*, pp. 136–8. If we look at the astronomical facts, as they were certainly known in Plato's day, and so, it is fair to presume, known to him, we may say that the planets have (a) a daily motion from east to west; (b) a longer-term motion, against the background of the fixed stars, from west to east; (c) certain motions (including retrogradation) peculiar to each, their observed motion not being simply the combined result of (a) and (b). (a) is, as we have seen, accounted for by the circle of the same, (b) *in general* by the motion of the circle of the different, but there are variations in the speeds of particular planets (36d). In the earlier passage it was assumed that the Sun, Mercury (Hermes) and Venus (Morning Star) moved as a group. We are now told that this is not so; they 'overtake and are overtaken by each other'. 'Venus and Mercury, though never far from the Sun, sometimes get ahead of him and appear as morning stars, sometimes drop behind, as evening stars' (Cornford, p. 106). They complete their journey through the signs of the Zodiac in a solar year, and in that sense can be grouped with the sun; but they are not always in the same relative positions, 'like a group of racers who reach the goal together, but on the way now one, now another is in front' (Cornford, p. 106). It is this variation of position for which the 'contrary power' is brought into account. And it seems plausible (with Cornford) to regard it as accounting also for the variations of speed already

mentioned, and for the retrogradations of the outer planets, whose motions are referred to in the next sentence only to be dismissed. Plato does not mention retrogradation, but he is at pains to emphasize in several places that there are more complications in the planetary movements than he can deal with in the context; Eudoxus, who was working in the Academy at about this time, certainly knew of it, and it seems reasonable to suppose that Plato knew too. We thus get a neat threefold scheme. The circle of the same accounts for the daily rotation; the circle of the different for the longer-term, west to east, motion; while the 'contrary power' accounts for all differences of speed or other peculiarities.

20.  Reading *iousan* and *kratoumenên* in 39a1.

21.  This sentence makes two points: (1) that the real movements are not the same as the apparent movements; the moon, for example, which seems to move 'most slowly', is really moving fastest (Cornford, *Cosmology*, p. 113); (2) that the combination of the motions of same and different, which are in different planes, produces a path which if traced on a sphere of the same radius is spiral (Cornford, p. 114).

22.  Reading *kath' ha* in 39b3.

23.  This so-called Great Year, completed when all the heavenly bodies came back to the same relative position.

24.  In Greek, *kosmos*. (TJ)

25.  I have retained the Oxford Classical Text reading *illomenên*, which Lee translates here as 'winding' and defends for the reasons given by Cornford, *Cosmology*, pp. 120 ff. However, the reader should be aware of how controversial the ascription of any movement to the Earth is. For a cogent defence of the alternative reading 'packed around' (*eillomenên*), which does not require the Earth to move, cf. D. J. Zeyl, *Timaeus*, pp. xlix–l. (TJ)

26.  The translation is highly contested; for a defence of the construal adopted here, see F. Karfik, *Die Beseelung des Kosmos*, pp. 87–148. (TJ)

27.  The word translated here as 'the whole' (*to pan*) is also Greek for 'the universe'. (TJ)

28.  'Sensation', *aisthêsis*, is here probably supposed to be derived from *aissô*, a verb meaning 'to move rapidly'.

29.  'Deflection' (*klasis*) is a term used specifically in geometry for the deflection of one line against another or in optics for the deflection of light against a surface (cf. Aristotle, *Physics* 228b24,

*Meteorology* 343a14, 373a5). Its use here underscores Timaeus' geometrical conception of the interaction between the linear bodily motions and the circular psychic motions. (TJ)

30. Timaeus is using the language of the Mysteries, initiation into which served to promote a happy afterlife; thus the word 'incomplete' (*atelês*) could also be translated 'uninitiated'. (TJ)

31. Colour vision is dealt with later at 67c–68d. (TJ)

32. 'that give us light' (*phôsphora*) is a rare epithet, but used of the eyes twice in Euripides' *Cyclops* (462, 611). For its significance here, see T. Johansen, *Plato's Natural Philosophy*, p. 114. (TJ)

33. Or 'remembered when we have emerged into the waking world'.

34. What happens with a normal mirror-image may be roughly represented as follows:

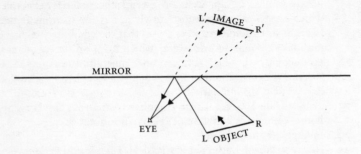

FIGURE 8 Mirror image. The example given of an object is the human face – Plato is thinking of looking at oneself in a mirror. When the mirror is concave the rays change sides, and if it is turned through a right angle the image appears upside-down.

35. The quotation – slightly adapted here – is from Euripides, *Phoenician Women* 1762. (TJ)

36. Reading *phônês* in 47d1.

37. The translation of the whole section is highly disputed. For an alternative translation, see H. Cherniss, 'A Much Misread Passage of the *Timaeus*'. On Cherniss' reading Timaeus is saying that we should not call the fleeting phenomenon (referred to as 'this') 'fire'; rather, we should call the recurrent formal quality (referred to as 'what is such') 'fire'. For critical discussion of Cherniss' alternative, see Zeyl, *Timaeus*, pp. lvi–lxiv. (TJ)

38. Omitting *kai tên tôide* in 49e3.

39. I take the thought to be that, given flux, fire is a recurrent quality ('what is continually such') rather than a stable continuous substance, as would be implied by calling it a 'this' or a 'this here'. (TJ)

40. Reading *tôi ta panta tôn noêtôn* in 51a1.

41. Timaeus here uses the word for 'man' that contrasts with 'woman'. (TJ)

42. Timaeus' thought seems to be that nothing that is properly speaking real comes into being in something else. So it is a sign of the tenuous grasp on being that the images enjoy that they only exist in so far as they come into being in something else, the receptacle; nothing similar applies to the eternal forms or the receptacle. People who think that to be real is to exist in some place are therefore as far as forms are concerned quite mistaken. Not distinguishing between what is true of the forms and what is true of the images they are in a sort of dream-like state. Cf. the dream-like state at *Republic* 476c–d of those who cannot distinguish between images and reality. (TJ)

43. Reading *mê* in 54b2.

44. The triangles are equilateral, so each solid angle contains 3 × 60° = 180°; the phrase 'the one which comes next after...' means the 'least angle which is not less than 180°', another way of saying that it is itself 180° (Taylor, *Commentary*, p. 375).

45. Reading *hôn peri* in 56c8.

46. This sentence gives the most precise formulation of the process by which one body changes into another. Using W, A, F for water, air and fire, we can say:

W = F + 2A, because in terms of basic triangles, 40 = 8 + (2 × 16)
A = 2F, because in terms of basic triangles, 16 = 2 × 8

For further analysis, see G. Vlastos, *Plato's Universe*, pp. 69 ff.

47. Reading *ean d'eis tauta iêi*.

48. There is an obscure play upon words in the Greek.

49. Cf. 68a below.

50. The parallel with Aristotle (*Meteorology* 383b9) suggests that the meaning is 'lava'.

51. Reading *kata nomon* in 60e1.

52. It seems that Timaeus, at first, uses the term *pathos* ('affection') for the effect that the bodies have on us in leading to perception, and *pathêma* ('attribute') for the property of bodies in virtue of

which we perceive them as being such and such. However, the terminological distinction is blurred, particularly from 65b on, and impossible to maintain in translation. One justification for the blurring may be that the attributes of bodies are identified on the basis of effects on our bodies that are such as to lead to perception. So hot, for example, is an attribute that bodies have in so far as they cut our bodies in a way that leads to perception of heat. This is as we would expect given Timaeus' introductory warning that the perceptual affections can be understood only in relation to the body and vice versa. Accordingly, I have translated both *pathos* and *pathêma* by 'affection', reserving 'attribute' for those occasions where Timaeus seems to have in mind specifically the condition of an *object* which may affect us. (TJ)

53. A play upon words in the Greek.

54. Cf. 80a below.

55. There is a transition here from the blending of light to the mixing of pigments. Greek colour words are sometimes hard to identify; the Greeks seem to have looked at the colour spectrum in a way different from ours. Aristotle deals with the colours of the rainbow in *Meteorology* 374b7–375a29 (and with colour mixtures more generally in *Sense and Sensibilia* 3. On the colour vocabulary of Ancient Greek, and comparisons with other cultures, see G. Lloyd, *Cognitive Variations* (Oxford, 2007), ch. 1 (TJ)).

56. The word Plato uses here for 'timber' (*hulê*) is the term we often translate as 'matter' (in contrast to 'form') in Aristotle. There are signs that the term already in Plato is assuming such a meaning (cf. *Philebus* 54c2); however, in the current context the reference to 'a carpenter' makes 'timber' the preferable translation. (TJ)

57. Reading *diulasmena* at 69a7. (TJ)

58. The image of a story as an animal with a body and a head is common in Plato, cf. *Gorgias* 505c, *Phaedrus* 264c. (TJ)

59. In Greek the words for 'brain' and 'head' are similar.

60. For the conflict between the motions of nutrition and the rational revolutions of the soul, cf. 43a. (TJ)

61. By 'the divine' Timaeus is probably thinking of the gods who are constructing the head, cf. the reference to 'Our maker' at 76c. (TJ)

62. Reading *phusei* with the manuscripts.

63. Cf. 75c–d.

64. The material of the 'network' is fire and air which can pass in and out through the pores of the flesh, which is made of coarser material. And in some way not easy to visualize in detail, the inner parts of the network are made of fire, the outer parts of air.
65. Cf. 47c–d.
66. The use of political terminology here and elsewhere invites the reader to draw analogies between the causes of order and disorder in the body and the city. (TJ)
67. Reading *kholôdes* at 83b6.
68. Reading *auto ekeinôn hama kai neurôn* in 84a2. (TJ)
69. A form of spasm in which the head and the heels are bent backward and the body bowed forward. (TJ)
70. 'Sacred malady' was a common name for epilepsy.
71. An implicit reference to the Greek phrase *kalokagathos* (a 'fine man' or 'gentleman'). (TJ)
72. See 51a, 52d–53a. (TJ)

# CRITIAS

1. A reference to dramatic competitions at Athens.
2. The Greek version of the English proverb 'nothing ventured, nothing gained'.
3. Cf. *Timaeus* 25d.
4. Cf. *Timaeus* 22d–23a.
5. The study of myths and research into ancient history are here treated like persons making a visit. For a similar explanation of the emergence of mathematical sciences in Egypt, see Aristotle, *Metaphysics* I.1.981b. (TJ)
6. An apparent reference to the joint rule of men and women in the ideal city, cf. *Timaeus* 18c and *Republic* 471d, 540c. (TJ)
7. Cf. *Timaeus* 17c–19a.
8. Cf. *Timaeus* 22a–b, 23a–c.
9. A reference to a Greek proverb, 'friends share all things in common'.
10. That is, midway along its greatest length.
11. A stade (*stadion*) is about 606 feet or 185 metres. (TJ)
12. Present-day Cadiz. (TJ)
13. The contrast is between solid materials like stone and marble and 'fusible' substances, i.e., in the main, metals.

14. Literally, 'mountain-copper'. The metal, whose identity is uncertain, is mentioned in the Hesiodic *Shield of Heracles* 122. (TJ)

15.

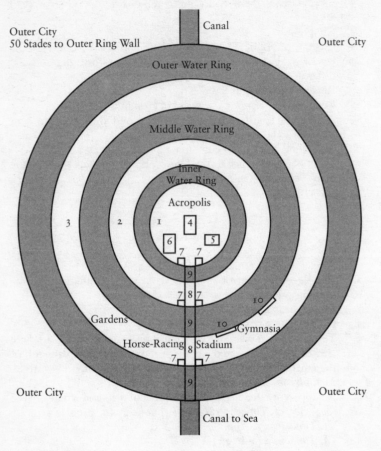

Outer City
50 Stades to Outer Ring Wall

Canal

Outer City

Outer Water Ring

Middle Water Ring

Inner
Water Ring

Acropolis

3          2          1          4

6          5

7    7

9

7  8  7

10

Gardens

10

9                    Gymnasia

Horse-Racing    8   Stadium

7          7

9

Outer City                                           Outer City

Canal to Sea

| 1 Central Island | 4 Shrine | 7 Towers and gates | 10 Docks |
| 2 Smaller ring-island | 5 Springs | 8 Covered channels | |
| 3 Larger ring-island | 6 Palace | 9 Bridges | |

FIGURE 9  The city and the buildings.

16.

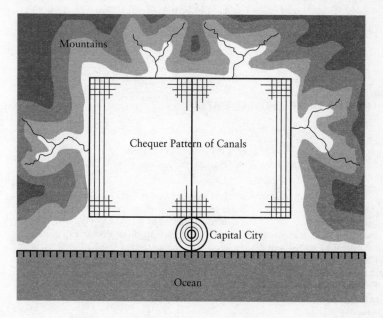

FIGURE 10 The canal pattern.

17. Length 3,000, breadth 2,000 (see 118a): 5,000 × 2 = 10,000.
18. Through the canal running through the city (see Figure 9 above).
19. Following the construal of L. Brisson, *Platon. Timée, Critias* (Paris, 1999), p. 374. (TJ)

# PENGUIN CLASSICS

**THE RISE OF THE ROMAN EMPIRE**
POLYBIUS

> 'If history is deprived of the truth,
> we are left with nothing but an idle, unprofitable tale'

In writing his account of the relentless growth of the Roman Empire, the Greek statesman Polybius (*c*. 200–118 BC) set out to help his fellow-countrymen understand how their world came to be dominated by Rome. Opening with the Punic War in 264 BC, he vividly records the critical stages of Roman expansion: its campaigns throughout the Mediterranean, the temporary setbacks inflicted by Hannibal and the final destruction of Carthage in 146 BC. An active participant in contemporary politics, as well as a friend of many prominent Roman citizens, Polybius was able to draw on a range of eyewitness accounts and on his own experiences of many of the central events, giving his work immediacy and authority.

Ian Scott-Kilvert's translation fully preserves the clarity of Polybius' narrative. This substantial selection of the surviving volumes is accompanied by an introduction by F. W. Walbank, which examines Polybius' life and times, and the sources and technique he employed in writing his history.

Translated by Ian Scott-Kilvert
Selected with an introduction by F. W. Walbank

# PENGUIN CLASSICS

**CONVERSATIONS OF SOCRATES**
XENOPHON

Socrates' Defence/Memoirs of Socrates/The Estate-Manager/The Dinner-Party

'He seemed to me to be the perfect example of goodness and happiness'

After the execution of Socrates in 399 BC, a number of his followers wrote dialogues featuring him as the protagonist and, in so doing, transformed the great philosopher into a legendary figure. Xenophon's portrait is the only one other than Plato's to survive, and while it offers a very personal interpretation of Socratic thought, it also reveals much about the man and his philosophical views. In 'Socrates' Defence' Xenophon defends his mentor against charges of arrogance made at his trial, while the 'Memoirs of Socrates' also starts with an impassioned plea for the rehabilitation of a wronged reputation. Along with 'The Estate-Manager', a practical economic treatise, and 'The Dinner-Party', a sparkling exploration of love, Xenophon's dialogues offer fascinating insights into the Socratic world and into the intellectual atmosphere and daily life of ancient Greece.

Xenophon's complete Socratic works are translated in this volume. In his introduction, Robin Waterfield illuminates the significance of these four books, showing how perfectly they embody the founding principles of Socratic thought.

Translated by Hugh Tredennick and Robin Waterfield and edited with new material by Robin Waterfield

# PENGUIN CLASSICS

**ELECTRA AND OTHER PLAYS**
SOPHOCLES

Ajax/Electra/Women of Trachis/Philoctetes

> 'Now that he is dead,
> I turn to you; will you be brave enough
> To help me kill the man who killed our father?'

Sophocles' innovative plays transformed Greek myths into dramas featuring complex human characters, through which he explored profound moral issues. *Electra* portrays the grief of a young woman for her father Agamemnon, who has been killed by her mother's lover. Aeschylus and Euripides also dramatized this story, but the objectivity and humanity of Sophocles' version provided a new perspective. Depicting the fall of a great hero, *Ajax* examines the enigma of power and weakness combined in one being, while the *Women of Trachis* portrays the tragic love and error of Heracles' deserted wife Deianeira, and *Philoctetes* deals with the conflict between physical force and moral strength.

E. F. Watling's vivid translation is accompanied by an introduction in which he discusses Sophocles' use of a third actor to create new dramatic situations and compares the different treatments of the Electra myth by the three great tragic poets of classical Athens.

Translated with an introduction by E. F. Watling

# PENGUIN CLASSICS

## THE GREEK SOPHISTS

'In the case of wisdom, those who sell it to anyone who wants it are called sophists'

By mid-fifth century BC, Athens was governed by democratic rule and power turned upon the ability of the individual to command the attention of the other citizens, and to sway the crowds of the assembly. It was the Sophists who understood the art of rhetoric and the importance of being able to transform effective reasoning into persuasive public speaking. Their inquiries – into the gods, the origins of religion and whether virtue can be taught – laid the groundwork for the next generation of thinkers such as Plato and Aristotle.

Each chapter of *The Greek Sophists* is based around the work of one character: Gorgias, Prodicus, Protagoras and Antiphon among others, and a linking commentary, chronological table and bibliography are provided for each one. In his introduction, John Dillon discusses the historical background and the sources of the text.

Translated by John Dillon and Tania Gergel with an introduction by John Dillon

# PENGUIN CLASSICS

**THE AGRICOLA *AND* THE GERMANIA**
TACITUS

> 'Happy indeed were you, Agricola,
> not only in your glorious life but in your timely death'

*The Agricola* is both a portrait of Julius Agricola – the most famous governor of Roman Britain and Tacitus' well-loved and respected father-in-law – and the first detailed account of Britain that has come down to us. It offers fascinating descriptions of the geography, climate and peoples of the country, and a succinct account of the early stages of the Roman occupation, nearly fatally undermined by Boudicca's revolt in AD 61 but consolidated by campaigns that took Agricola as far as Anglesey and northern Scotland. The warlike German tribes are the focus of Tacitus' attention in *The Germania*, which, like *The Agricola*, often compares the behaviour of 'barbarian' peoples favourably with the decadence and corruption of Imperial Rome.

Harold Mattingly's translation brings Tacitus' extravagant imagination and incisive wit vividly to life. In his introduction, he examines Tacitus' life and literary career, the governorship of Agricola, and the political background of Rome's rapidly expanding Empire. This edition also includes a select bibliography, and maps of Roman Britain and Germany.

Translated with an introduction by H. Mattingly
Translation revised by S. A. Handford

## THE ALEXIAD OF ANNA COMNENA

'The shining light of the world, the great Alexius'

Anna Comnena (1083–1153) wrote *The Alexiad* as an account of the reign of her father, the Byzantine Emperor Alexius I. It is also an important source of information on the Byzantine war with the Normans, and on the First Crusade in which Alexius participated. While the Byzantines were allied to the Crusaders, they were nonetheless critical of their behaviour and Anna's book offers a startlingly different perspective to that of Western historians. Her character sketches are shrewd and forthright – from the Norman invader Robert Guiscard ('nourished by manifold evil') and his son Bohemond ('like a streaking thunderbolt') to Pope Gregory VII ('unworthy of a high priest'). *The Alexiad* is a vivid and dramatic narrative, which reveals as much about the character of its intelligent and dynamic author as it does about the fascinating period through which she lived.

E. R. A. Sewter's translation captures all the strength and immediacy of the original and is complimented by an introduction, which examines Anna's life and times. This edition also includes maps, appendices, genealogical tables, a bibliography, and indexes of events and names.

Translated with an introduction by E. R. A. Sewter

# Penguin Classics

**CITY OF GOD**
ST AUGUSTINE

> 'The Heavenly City outshines Rome, beyond comparison.
> There, instead of victory, is truth; instead of rank, holiness'

St Augustine, bishop of Hippo, was one of the central figures in the history of
Christianity, and *City of God* is one of his greatest theological works. Written as an
eloquent defence of the faith at a time when the Roman Empire was on the brink
of collapse, it examines the ancient pagan religions of Rome, the arguments of the
Greek philosophers and the revelations of the Bible. Pointing the way forward to
a citizenship that transcends the best political experiences of the world and offers
citizenship that will last for eternity, *City of God* is one of the most influential
documents in the development of Christianity.

This edition contains a new introduction that examines the text in the light of
contemporary Greek and Roman thought and political change, and demonstrates
the religious and literary influences on St Augustine and his significance as a
Christian thinker. There is also a chronology and bibliography.

Translated with notes by Henry Bettenson with an introduction by Gill Evans

# PENGUIN CLASSICS

**THE FROGS AND OTHER PLAYS**
ARISTOPHANES

The Wasps/The Poet and the Women/The Frogs

> 'This is just a little fable, with a moral: not too highbrow for you, we hope,
> but a bit more intelligent than the usual knockabout stuff'

The master of ancient Greek comic drama, Aristophanes combined slapstick, humour and cheerful vulgarity with acute political observations. In *The Frogs*, written during the Peloponnesian War, Dionysus descends to the Underworld to bring back a poet who can help Athens in its darkest hour, and stages a great debate to help him decide between the traditional wisdom of Aeschylus and the brilliant modernity of Euripides. The clash of generations and values is also the object of Aristophanes' satire in *The Wasps*, in which an old-fashioned father and his loose-living son come to blows and end up in court. And in *The Poet and the Women*, Euripides, accused of misogyny, persuades a relative to infiltrate an all-women festival to find out whether revenge is being plotted against him.

David Barrett's introduction discusses the Athenian dramatic contests in which these plays first appeared, and conventions of Greek comedy – from its poetic language and the role of the Chorus to casting and costumes.

Translated with an introduction by David Barrett

# PENGUIN CLASSICS

---

**THE HISTORY OF THE DECLINE & FALL OF THE ROMAN EMPIRE**
EDWARD GIBBON

> 'Instead of inquiring why the Roman empire was destroyed,
> we should rather be surprised that it had subsisted so long'

Edward Gibbon's *Decline and Fall of the Roman Empire* compresses thirteen
turbulent centuries into an epic narrative shot through with insight, irony and
incisive character analysis. Sceptical about Christianity, sympathetic to the
barbarian invaders and the Byzantine Empire, constantly aware of how political
leaders often achieve the exact opposite of what they intend, Gibbon was alert both
to the broad pattern of events and to significant revealing details. The first of its
six volumes, published in 1776, was attacked for its enlightened views on politics,
sexuality and religion, yet it was an immediate bestseller and widely acclaimed
for the elegance of its prose. Gripping, powerfully intelligent and wonderfully
entertaining, it is among the greatest works of history in the English language and
a literary masterpiece of its age.

This abridgement is based on David Womersley's definitive three-volume Penguin
Classics edition of *Decline and Fall of the Roman Empire*. Complete chapters
from each volume, linked by extended bridging passages, vividly capture the style,
argument and structure of the whole work.

Edited and abridged by David Womersley

---

# PENGUIN CLASSICS

**THE REPUBLIC**
**PLATO**

*'We are concerned with the most important of issues, the choice between a good and an evil life'*

Plato's *Republic* is widely acknowledged as the cornerstone of Western philosophy. Presented in the form of a dialogue between Socrates and three different interlocutors, it is an inquiry into the notion of a perfect community and the ideal individual within it. During the conversation other questions are raised: what is goodness; what is reality; what is knowledge? *The Republic* also addresses the purpose of education and the roles of both women and men as 'guardians' of the people. With remarkable lucidity and deft use of allegory, Plato arrives at a depiction of a state bound by harmony and ruled by 'philosopher kings'.

Desmond Lee's translation of *The Republic* has come to be regarded as a classic in its own right. The new introduction by Melissa Lane discusses Plato's aims in writing *The Republic*, its major arguments and perspective on politics in ancient Greece, and its significance through the ages and today.

Translated with an introduction by Desmond Lee

# PENGUIN CLASSICS

**THE POLITICS**
ARISTOTLE

'Man is by nature a political animal'

In *The Politics* Aristotle addresses the questions that lie at the heart of political science. How should society be ordered to ensure the happiness of the individual? Which forms of government are best and how should they be maintained? By analysing a range of city constitutions – oligarchies, democracies and tyrannies – he seeks to establish the strengths and weaknesses of each system to decide which are the most effective, in theory and in practice. A hugely significant work, which has influenced thinkers as diverse as Aquinas and Machiavelli, *The Politics* remains an outstanding commentary on fundamental political issues and concerns, and provides fascinating insights into the workings and attitudes of the Greek city-state.

The introductions by T. A. Sinclair and Trevor J. Saunders discuss the influence of *The Politics* on philosophers, its modern relevance and Aristotle's political beliefs. This edition contains Greek and English glossaries, and a bibliography for further reading.

Translated by T. A. Sinclair
Revised and re-presented by Trevor J. Saunders

# PENGUIN CLASSICS

**THE PERSIAN EXPEDITION**
XENOPHON

'The only things of value which we have at present are our arms and our courage'

In *The Persian Expedition*, Xenophon, a young Athenian noble who sought his destiny abroad, provides an enthralling eyewitness account of the attempt by a Greek mercenary army – the Ten Thousand – to help Prince Cyrus overthrow his brother and take the Persian throne. When the Greeks were then betrayed by their Persian employers, they were forced to march home through hundreds of miles of difficult terrain – adrift in a hostile country and under constant attack from the unforgiving Persians and warlike tribes. In this outstanding description of endurance and individual bravery, Xenophon, one of those chosen to lead the retreating army, provides a vivid narrative of the campaign and its aftermath, and his account remains one of the best pictures we have of Greeks confronting a 'barbarian' world.

Rex Warner's distinguished translation captures the epic quality of the Greek original and George Cawkwell's introduction sets the story of the expedition in the context of its author's life and tumultuous times.

Translated by Rex Warner with an introduction by George Cawkwell

# PENGUIN CLASSICS

**MEDEA AND OTHER PLAYS**
EURIPIDES

Medea/Alcestis/The Children of Heracles/Hippolytus

'That proud, impassioned soul,
so ungovernable now that she has felt the sting of injustice'

*Medea,* in which a spurned woman takes revenge upon her lover by killing her children, is one of the most shocking and horrific of all the Greek tragedies. Dominating the play is Medea herself, a towering and powerful figure who demonstrates Euripides' unusual willingness to give voice to a woman's case. *Alcestis,* a tragicomedy, is based on a magical myth in which Death is overcome, and *The Children of Heracles* examines the conflict between might and right, while *Hippolytus* deals with self-destructive integrity and moral dilemmas. These plays show Euripides transforming the awesome figures of Greek mythology into recognizable, fallible human beings.

John Davie's accessible prose translation is accompanied by a general introduction and individual prefaces to each play.

'John Davie's translations are outstanding ... the tone throughout is refreshingly modern yet dignified' William Allan, *Classical Review*

Previously published as *Alcestis and Other Plays*.

Translated by John Davie, with an introduction and notes by Richard Rutherford